CW01192081

Marvellous Messages

I dedicate this book to the lack of education on deaf history, which inspired me to create something for your bookshelf at home.

Rose Ayling-Ellis

Marvellous Messages

Illustrated by Lena Addink

Rose Ayling-Ellis

DK

CONTENTS

Wow... look at all the places we're going, Perky!

6	A letter from Rose
8	The adventure begins...
10	**STOP 01:** Olympic Stadium, Greece
12	**STOP 02:** Ancient Rome
14	**STOP 03:** Rome, Italy
16	**STOP 04:** Leicestershire, England
18	**Rose's Superstars:** Kitty O'Neil
20	**STOP 05:** Deaf school, England
22	**STOP 06:** Coral reef, Indian Ocean
24	**STOP 07:** Paris, France
26	**Rose's Superstars:** Cliff Bastin
28	**STOP 08:** Calligraphy studio, China
30	**Messaging Milestones:** Printing
32	**STOP 09:** Valley of the Kings, Egypt
34	**STOP 10:** Baghdad, Persia (now Iran)
36	**Rose's Superstars:** Thomas Edison
38	**STOP 11:** Isle of Iona, Scotland
40	**STOP 12:** Paris, France
42	**Messaging Milestones:** Telephone
44	**STOP 13:** Great Plains of North America
46	**STOP 14:** Maasai Mara, Kenya
48	**STOP 15:** International Airport, Hong Kong

50	**Rose's Superstars:**	Ruth Montgomery
52	**STOP 16:**	Hawai'i, Pacific Ocean
54	**STOP 17:**	Honey farm, Türkiye
56	**STOP 18:**	Lyceum, Ancient Greece
58	**STOP 19:**	Glass workshop, Venice
60	**Messaging Milestones:**	Television
62	**STOP 20:**	Buckingham Palace, England
64	**Rose's Superstars:**	Haben Girma
66	**STOP 21:**	Puppy school, Wales
68	**STOP 22:**	Johannesburg, South Africa
70	**STOP 23:**	London, England
72	**Rose's Superstars:**	Millicent Simmonds
74	**STOP 24:**	Chicago, USA
76	**Messaging Milestones:**	Written Messages
78	**STOP 25:**	New York City, USA
80	**Rose's Superstars:**	Being Her
82	**STOP 26:**	Oxford, England
84	**STOP 27:**	Space, orbiting Earth
86	**Messaging Milestones:**	Digital World
88	**STOP 28:**	Outer space
90	**STOP 29:**	Rose's home
92	Glossary	
94	Index	
96	Acknowledgements	

Yes! Buckle up readers, Perky Pilot is ready for take-off!

STOP 00
DESTINATION
DATE TODAY!
29-STAGE WORLD TOUR
TAKE OFF FOR TIME TRAVEL!
PERKY PILOT AIRWAYS

Hello!

My name is Rose, and I'm an actress from England. When I'm not working, I love spending time with my family and friends. My favourite things are arts, gardening, performing – and cats! (Even though I am allergic to them but shh...! No one needs to know, especially not my favourite cats in the world – Casper, Halo, and Rocky!)

What else? Oh yes! I was born deaf. Growing up deaf in a hearing world was challenging at times, but I wouldn't have it any other way. My deafness has played a big part in making me who I am. I was lucky to learn British Sign Language (BSL) as a child. I know I'm biased, but I believe sign language is the world's most expressive and beautiful language! People assume that communication means only listening and speaking. But what if I could show you that there are thousands of different ways to communicate? My deafness and BSL has taught me that communicating is about so much more than words.

That's why I decided to write this book – to share my experience of all the incredible ways we can connect with each other. You'll join me on my epic adventure, crossing continents and travelling through time as

Casper, Halo, and Rocky

Flick through the pages to make Perky's pal, Pablo, fly!

Perky the magical pigeon flies us around the world — and beyond! You'll discover how people, past and present, learned to be awesome communicators. You'll see the clever ways we did it long before smartphones and social media, and be amazed at how we always find a way to connect, even in the trickiest situations.

I would have loved to have read a book like this when I was younger. I grew up not seeing any deaf role models or learning about the brilliant things they had achieved. So in this book, you'll also find out about some deaf people who have made a real difference to our world. I'm so glad to give you the chance to meet a few of the people who are total superstars in my eyes!

Being seen and understood is what makes each and every one of us feel heard. I hope this book gives you the confidence and courage to express yourself in your own way, and inspires you to find ways to connect with people who may not communicate in the same way as you. And remember — anything is possible, so follow your dreams!

Come on, what are you waiting for? Let's go!

Rose x

Flick through the pages to make Perky's pal, Pippa, fly!

THE ADVENTURE BEGINS...

"**What a day!**" Rose said. Halo the cat jumped on her lap, while Rocky and Casper carried on sleeping.

All day, Rose had been interrupted by video calls, emails, and texts. She hadn't got anything done. Enough was enough. She turned off all her devices and flopped down on the sofa. Peace at last!

Dev, her sign language interpreter, sat down beside her. "Tell me about it!" he signed.

"Why do we need all this digital stuff, anyway?" Rose signed to Dev. "They didn't have it in the past, but still managed to get by. I wish… I WISH… I was somewhere it had never been invented!"

Suddenly, Dev looked up and pointed to the window. Rose looked over – and she couldn't believe her eyes. Pecking at the glass was a pigeon, and he was wearing a fancy green waistcoat! Rose opened the window and the pigeon flew in.

"Perky Pigeon, here to make your wish come true!" he proclaimed in a booming voice, as Dev interpreted in sign language for Rose.

"My wish?" repeated Rose, her eyes wide. Halo eyed the pigeon with an expression somewhere between fear and hunger. Still, Rocky and Casper continued sleeping.

"You made a wish for a world without digital devices, so I'm going to grant you that wish," explained Perky. "I'm a rather magical pigeon, you see. I can go anywhere – even back in time. You're going on a trip with Perky Pilot Airways."

"Perky… what?" Rose repeated in disbelief.

"Here are your boarding passes," Perky said. "We'll make stops all over the world, past and present, to look at some cool ways to communicate with not a smartphone in sight! The route might seem a little random, but you'll get the message by the end. All you need to do is hop on my back."

"I don't think we'll all fit," said Rose.

"A-ha! That's where the magic happens. Rub my wing, stand back, and watch!"

Rose gave Perky's wing a nervous rub and… **WHOOSH!** Immediately, the air filled with smoke and sparkles. Perky became the size of a little plane! His whopping wings were flapping up and down at high speed.

"Time for take off," announced Pilot Perky, putting on a smart pilot's cap.

Rose, Halo, and Dev all climbed aboard and in a flash, they were soaring through the night sky. The rooftops grew smaller as the stars grew brighter. Below, the land became a distant blur as they flew faster and higher.

"This is my bird's-eye view of the world," said Pilot Perky with pride.

"And now it's my Rose-eye view!" replied Rose. "This adventure is going to be amazing! Where's our first stop?"

STOP **01** DESTINATION **OLYMPIC STADIUM, GREECE**

DATE **650 BCE**

TAKE OFF FOR TIME TRAVEL! PERKY PILOT AIRWAYS

Night turned to day. Pilot Perky flew lower and landed near a sports stadium bathed in sunshine. As soon as he touched down, Perky returned to his normal size and the passengers slid off his back, landing in a heap.

"Where are we?" asked Rose, holding Halo up so she could get a better look.

"Welcome to ancient Greece – and the Olympic Games!"

"So why are we here?" Rose asked him.

Fluffing up his feathers, Perky said, "I don't want to boast, but at these games, pigeons like me delivered the world's first text messages. Every athlete had his own homing pigeon. If he won an event, he wrote a message for the pigeon to carry back to his home village so they could prepare a hero's welcome for him."

"That's so cool," said Rose. Then suddenly she yelled, "Look, those runners aren't wearing anything!"

Halo covered her eyes with her paws.

"Robes would just slow the runners down," explained Perky. "At the ancient Olympics, all the athletes competed naked!"

"What kind of sports did they have?" Rose asked.

"Mainly running races. Then there was wrestling, boxing, and even chariot racing – if you could afford your own horses."

"Come on, let's get a seat to watch the next race," said Rose.

"Luckily for you, we're invisible when we visit the past," said Perky. "Women and girls weren't allowed to take part or even watch the Games.

GREAT GAMES

The first Olympic Games of modern times were in 1896, in Athens, Greece.

The Paralympics, for disabled athletes, were first held in 1960 in Rome, Italy.

In 1924, deaf competitors took part in the first Deaflympics in Paris, France.

You see Mount Olympus over there?"

Rose looked in the direction of the mighty peak.

"Well, any female caught at the Games would be taken there and thrown off the top of the mountain!"

Rose's jaw dropped. "Are you **SURE** we're invisible, Perky? Just in case...

"LET'S GET OUT OF HERE!"

STOP 02	DESTINATION
DATE	**ANCIENT ROME**
48 BCE	

TAKE OFF FOR TIME TRAVEL! — PERKY PILOT AIRWAYS

Pilot Perky became huge again and they took off, travelling so fast that everything passed by them in a blur. Rose felt a tingle of excitement. She loved speed! This time when they landed, they were all ready for the bump.

"Where are we now?" asked Rose.

"This is the city of Rome in ancient times – and that chap there is the Emperor, Julius Caesar!"

Rose stared in surprise as the leader of the Roman Empire wandered past, holding a letter in his hand.

"What's he reading?" wondered Rose.

"Let's have a look!" said Perky, who could never resist reading messages.

Rose looked over Caesar's shoulder and said, "It's just a jumble of letters. It doesn't make any sense."

"A-ha! That's because it's in code. Caesar invented one of the first-ever codes so he could send top-secret messages to his soldiers during battles. You have to know the code to work out what the message really says."

"Do you know how it works?" asked Rose.

"I do! Each letter moves the same number of spaces in the alphabet," said Perky.

Perky used his beak to draw out the letters in the dust. "You see?" he said. "If you move every letter in 'PERKY' forward by one, my name would be 'QFSLZ'."

"Amazing!" said Rose. "So what does Caesar's message say?

"It says 'VENI, VIDI, VICI'", replied Perky.

"But that still doesn't make sense to me," said Rose, looking perplexed.

Perky laughed. "It's Caesar's favourite saying, but it's in Latin, the language he spoke. It means '**I CAME, I SAW, I CONQUERED**'."

"How do you know Latin?" asked Rose, shaking her head in amazement.

"I know every language!" announced Perky, proudly. "Let's go to the next stop, and I'll show you."

And so, in a puff of smoke and a flurry of feathers, they were off again…

CAESAR'S SECRET

Caesar's code worked by replacing each letter in a message with another letter a set number of places further on in the alphabet. So with a shift of three places, you would write D instead of A, E would be B, and so on. The word "cat" would be written as "fdw".

The original letter is "m".

a	b	c	d	e	f	g	h	i	j	k	l	m	n	o	p	q	r	s	t	u	v	w	x	y	z
d	e	f	g	h	i	j	k	l	m	n	o	p	q	r	s	t	u	v	w	x	y	z	a	b	c

The "m" becomes "p" in code.

Use this grid to spell out your name in Caesar's code. Then write a secret message to your friends!

STOP **03** DESTINATION
DATE **ROME, ITALY**
2024

TAKE OFF FOR TIME TRAVEL! — PERKY PILOT AIRWAYS

"I recognize this place!" said Rose with a smile.

"Yes, we're still in Rome, where Julius Caesar lived, but today it's the capital of Italy!" replied Perky.

"So we're back in the present?" asked Rose.

"Yes – and that means everyone can see us. And even better, we can buy treats. I'm peckish!" said Perky.

The friends wandered through the streets. Cafés were spilling over with people enjoying a cool drink or a slice of pizza in the sunshine. Perky stopped at a stall selling ice creams.

"Buon giorno! Tre gelati, per favore," said Perky to the stallholder.

Dev signed to Rose, "Sorry, I didn't get that. I think he's speaking another language!"

"What did you say, Perky?" Dev asked.

"I'm speaking Italian and I ordered these for us!" said Perky, handing Rose and Dev an ice-cream cone each.

"What happened to Latin?" Rose asked in between licks.

Turn to page 96 to find out which languages are on the board!

Benvenuto!
Welcome!
Wilkommen!
いらっしゃいませ
Witamy!
Bienvenu!
¡Bienvenido!

14

"No one speaks it any more, so it's called a dead language," said Perky with a wave of his wing. "Italian developed from Latin into a language of its own."

Rose pointed to the sign in front of the ice-cream stall. "Look at all these different languages!" she said.

"And they all mean the same thing – WELCOME!" said Perky.

"Why are there so many different languages in the world?" asked Rose.

"In ancient times, most people didn't travel far from home," explained Perky. "Each community had their own language. They didn't meet many outsiders, so it didn't matter if nobody else understood what they were saying."

Suddenly Rose grabbed Perky's wing. "Can we add a stop to the schedule? I'd like to go back to an important time for my language."

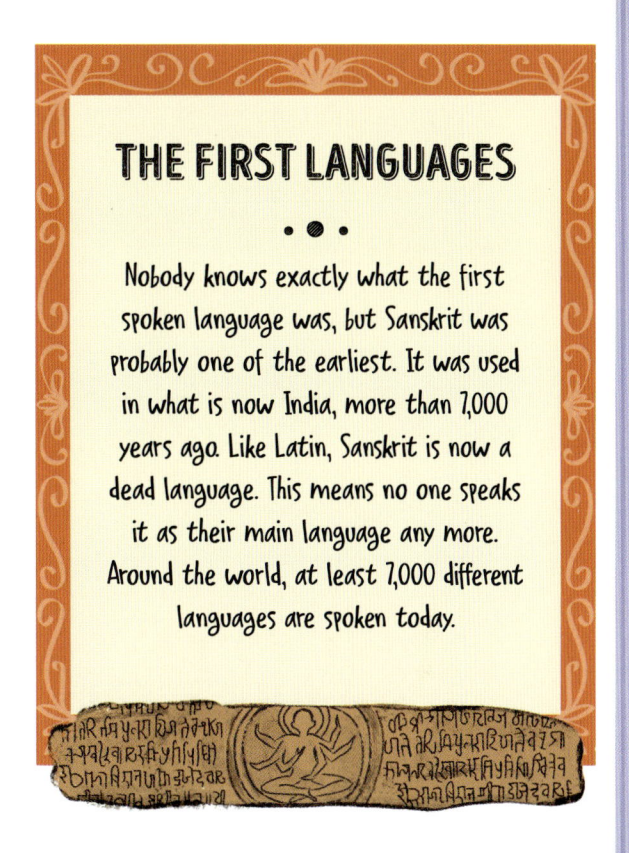

THE FIRST LANGUAGES

Nobody knows exactly what the first spoken language was, but Sanskrit was probably one of the earliest. It was used in what is now India, more than 7,000 years ago. Like Latin, Sanskrit is now a dead language. This means no one speaks it as their main language any more. Around the world, at least 7,000 different languages are spoken today.

"Marvellous idea!" bellowed Perky. "Hop on, team!"

"Ciao for now!" called Rose as they left Rome far below.

STOP 04 — **DESTINATION** LEICESTERSHIRE, ENGLAND
DATE 1576
TAKE OFF FOR TIME TRAVEL! — PERKY PILOT AIRWAYS

Pilot Perky whizzed the friends back through the centuries, faster and faster, until they came to a stop outside a church in an English village.

"The year, my friends, is 1576. Smarten up, we're off to a wedding!" said Perky.

As Perky preened his feathers and straightened his waistcoat, Halo licked the last of the ice cream off her paws.

"Wow, Perky, you did it! I've read about this moment, and now I'm going to see it," Rose said excitedly.

They entered the church and stood at the back to watch the ceremony. The groom, Thomas Tilsye, was sharing his vows with his bride, Ursula Russel. But Thomas wasn't talking. He was using sign language!

Thomas hugged Ursula, took her by the hand and put a ring on her finger. Ursula smiled back at him. Thomas laid his hand on Ursula's heart, then raised both hands upwards to heaven to show his love would last forever.

"You don't need to know sign language to understand that gesture," said Perky. "Thomas has so much love for Ursula."

Rose nodded in agreement. "Hands say so much. And faces, too!" she said.

"Ursula's eyes are shining with joy, aren't they? This wedding is so emotional."

Perky wiped his eye with his wing.

"Are you crying, Perky?" asked Rose.

"No, no! Something in my eye, that's all."

"Well, we've just witnessed a big moment!" said Rose. "This wedding was one of the first times on record when someone made their wedding vows in sign language."

At the end, Perky clapped his wings and Rose waved her hands with a twisting movement – the deaf applause sign.

"Now, at Rose's request, let's go and see how far sign language has come since then!" said Perky.

Off they flew to Stop 05 of Perky Pilot's Grand Tour…

Abbot (head of the abbey) **Provost** (deputy head) **Prior** (senior monk)

SILENT SIGNALS

In medieval times, monks who had vowed to stay silent used signs to communicate. Some signs are still used in British Sign Language today.

ANCIENT SIGNS

• •

The very first sign language that we know about dates back to the 5th century BCE, when the Greek philosopher Socrates described people who could not speak using head and hand gestures instead.

ROSE'S SUPERSTARS
KITTY O'NEIL

Fearless and fabulous, deaf stuntwoman and racing driver Kitty O'Neil lived life in the fast lane. She broke all kinds of records, earning the nickname "Fastest Woman in the World!"

THE JOURNEY BEGINS

Kitty was born in Texas, USA, in 1946. She became deaf after an illness when she was a baby. By the age of two she was learning to talk and lip-read. As a child, she loved music, and played the piano and cello. But more than anything, Kitty loved adventure. She tried all kinds of daredevil activities, including skydiving, hang-gliding, and scuba diving.

THE NEED FOR SPEED

Speedy Kitty set records on land, in water, and in the air. In 1976 she took the wheel of *Motivator*, a rocket-powered, three-wheeled vehicle. Racing over the desert in the US state of Oregon, Kitty set a new land-speed record. Then in 1977, she set a women's water-speed record in her jet-powered boat *Captain Crazy*. Even on water-skis, Kitty was a world-beater, setting a women's speed record in 1970.

LAND SPEED
1976
999 km/h
621 mph

WATER SPEED
1977
443 km/h
275 mph

WATER-SKIING
1970
169 km/h
105 mph

THRILLS AND SPILLS

Kitty's exploits led to a new career as a stunt performer, taking the place of actors for dangerous or difficult scenes. She became famous for her work on the TV shows *The Bionic Woman* and *Wonder Woman*. And still those records kept coming. Kitty leapt 39 m (128 ft) off a building to set a new high-fall stunt record. When she jumped 55 m (180 ft) from a helicopter, she described her view of the landing airbag as the size of a postage stamp!

> "I'm not afraid of anything. Just do it. It feels good when you finish. You made it!"
>
> KITTY O'NEIL

What an amazing woman, Perky!

Indeed she was. I almost flew into her once!

DARE TO DREAM

This real-life *Wonder Woman* became so famous that there was even a Kitty O'Neil action doll! Kitty said that her deafness was never an issue; in fact it was a benefit, as not hearing helped her stay focused on her goals. Kitty died in 2018, but her outstanding courage and commitment to achieving her dreams mean that she will never be forgotten.

KIT BITS

Kitty's mother founded a school for deaf students in the Texas town of Wichita Falls.

Kitty was only afraid of two things: spiders and mice!

STOP 05
DESTINATION: DEAF SCHOOL, ENGLAND
DATE: 2024
TAKE OFF FOR TIME TRAVEL!
PERKY PILOT AIRWAYS

BSL ALPHABET

A B C D E F G H I J K L M N O P Q R S T U V W X Y Z

"Here we are," said Perky after the usual bone-shaking landing. "Why did you want to come here, Rose?"

"This is a school for deaf children. As well as other subjects, they all learn BSL – British Sign Language!" said Rose.

Rose pointed to a poster. "BSL is an amazing language. Names and places are spelled by fingerspelling with two hands, but most words have their own sign. But we don't just sign with our hands – we use our faces and bodies, too!"

Rose showed them a sign, moving her hand down from her chin and away from her body.

"Easy," said Perky. "That means 'thank you'!"

"You're right!" said Rose.

"My wings may not be very good for signing, but I'm still excellent at understanding BSL, if I do say so myself," said Perky modestly.

"You're a marvel, Perky!" said Rose. "Have you got a sign name?"

"What's a sign name?" Perky asked, looking confused.

"We often have our own sign names. It's an easy way to identify someone without having to fingerspell their name," Rose explained.

"I'd love to have one!" said Perky.

"OK. You can be 'Flappy', and this is your sign," said Rose, flapping her hands like wings and bobbing her head.

"I like it," said Perky, copying Rose's actions.

Halo tapped Rose's arm with her paw. She wanted a sign name, too.

"Your sign name can be … 'Tapping'!" said Rose, touching the back of one hand with two fingers of the other. Halo looked pleased.

"There are other sign languages, and places where hearing people use signs, too," said Perky knowledgeably. "Hop aboard and I'll show you at the next stop!"

ALL ABOUT BSL

There are up to 100,000 different signs, and new ones are added regularly. In 2023, deaf scientists came up with 200 new signs to help them talk about climate change, including signs for "carbon footprint" and "greenhouse gas".

Now it's your turn! Use the BSL alphabet opposite to fingerspell your name and where you live.

HELLO/GOODBYE

PLEASE/THANKS

SORRY

STOP **06**

DATE
2024

DESTINATION

CORAL REEF, INDIAN OCEAN

TAKE OFF FOR TIME TRAVEL! — PERKY PILOT AIRWAYS

ARE YOU OK? I'M OK!

LOOK!

SEA SPEAK

∴

As well as hand signals, scuba divers also communicate using writing slates, digital devices, and waterproof torches.

The friends landed back in the present, on a beautiful beach. This was paradise!

"Perky, have you taken us all on holiday?" asked Rose, settling down on a sunlounger in the shade of a swaying palm tree. "What a treat!"

"Oh no, you don't," said Perky, waving his wing towards the ocean. "We're going in…"

Perky led everyone to a submarine at the water's edge. "Come on, come on, don't dilly-dally!"

In seconds, the submarine was powering through the water before sinking beneath the waves. Halo's whiskers twitched hungrily as she watched schools of fish pass the porthole. Soon they came to a colourful coral reef, where two scuba divers were busy exploring. One diver made a hand gesture to the other.

"Look," said Rose. "The divers are making signs. It looks a little bit like BSL!"

"You're right," said Perky. "Divers need to communicate, but talking is impossible – you'd end up with a lungful of water! Hand signals work much better."

HOLD HANDS

BREATHE

GO DOWN

GET WITH YOUR BUDDY

GO UP, END DIVE NOW

"They've spotted something," said Rose. Sure enough, one diver was using a signal to show his partner where to look to spot a passing green turtle.

They watched as the divers used different signals to communicate with each other.

"I never thought about it, but deaf divers who sign can communicate underwater much better than most people," said Rose.

"In fact, you could say deaf divers have IN-DEPTH conversations!" said Perky, who laughed while everyone else groaned.

"You and your terrible 'hearing' jokes, Perky," said Rose, shaking her head. "But thank you for reminding me how useful signing can be – even under the sea!"

SIGN OF THE TIMES

• •

There are more than 300 different types of sign language in use around the world today.

23

STOP 07

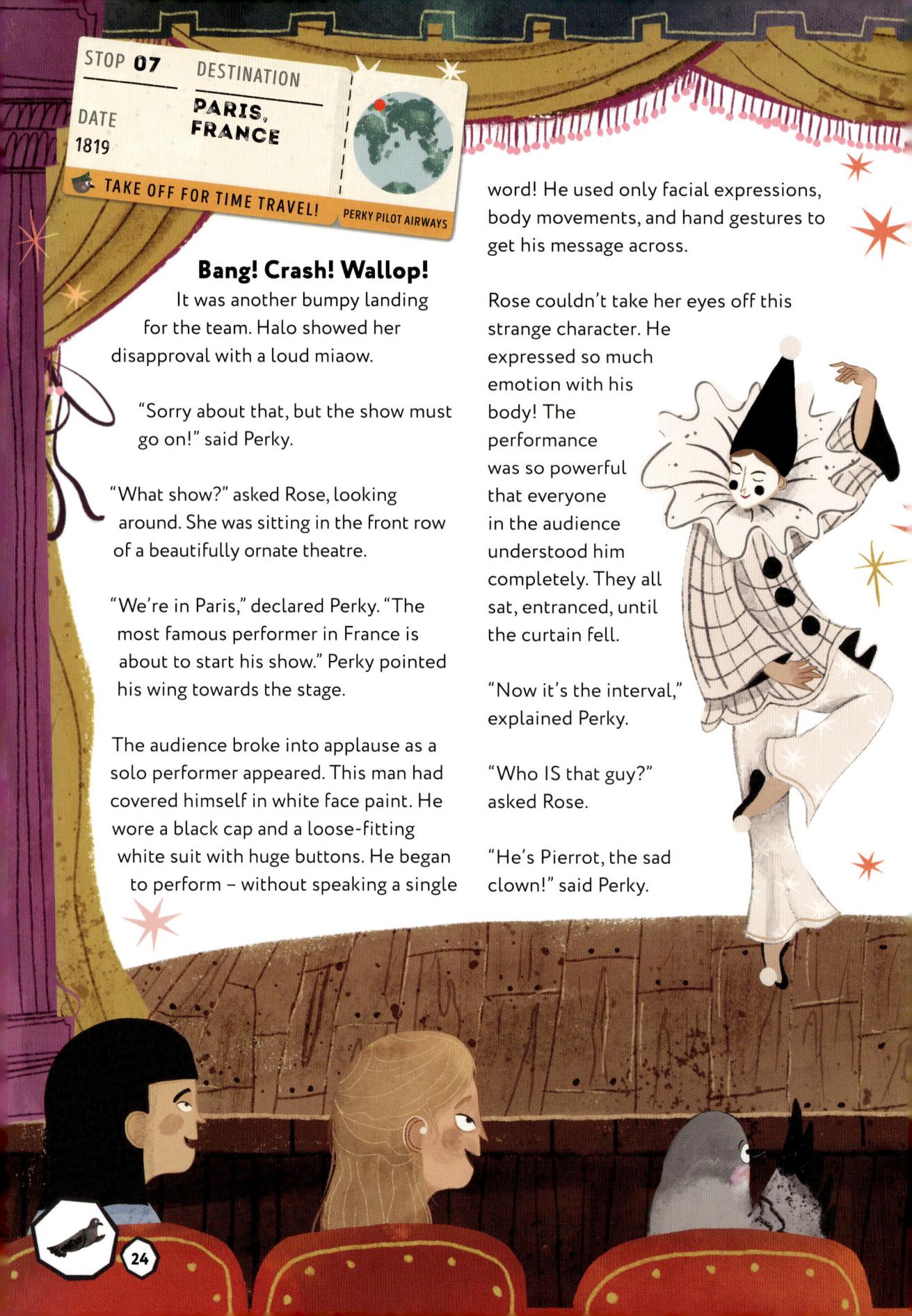

DESTINATION
PARIS, FRANCE

DATE
1819

TAKE OFF FOR TIME TRAVEL!

PERKY PILOT AIRWAYS

Bang! Crash! Wallop!

It was another bumpy landing for the team. Halo showed her disapproval with a loud miaow.

"Sorry about that, but the show must go on!" said Perky.

"What show?" asked Rose, looking around. She was sitting in the front row of a beautifully ornate theatre.

"We're in Paris," declared Perky. "The most famous performer in France is about to start his show." Perky pointed his wing towards the stage.

The audience broke into applause as a solo performer appeared. This man had covered himself in white face paint. He wore a black cap and a loose-fitting white suit with huge buttons. He began to perform – without speaking a single word! He used only facial expressions, body movements, and hand gestures to get his message across.

Rose couldn't take her eyes off this strange character. He expressed so much emotion with his body! The performance was so powerful that everyone in the audience understood him completely. They all sat, entranced, until the curtain fell.

"Now it's the interval," explained Perky.

"Who IS that guy?" asked Rose.

"He's Pierrot, the sad clown!" said Perky.

24

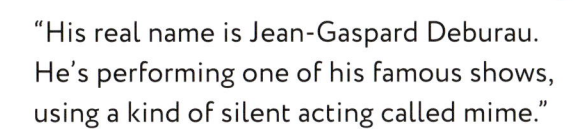

"His real name is Jean-Gaspard Deburau. He's performing one of his famous shows, using a kind of silent acting called mime."

"Did he invent it?" asked Rose.

"No! Mime is an ancient art. But Deburau brought it up to date with his Pierrot character, who was loved by audiences. Thanks to him, mime became all the rage here in France and all over Europe," answered Perky.

Rose's eyes shone as Pierrot returned to the stage for the second part of the show. He was utterly spellbinding! At the end, everyone stood and cheered the star.

"A little birdie told me you've received standing ovations at the theatre, too…" said Perky to Rose.

"Perky, how do you know so many things?" said Rose, looking surprised. "You're right, I have! In 2023 I was in a play called *As You Like It*, by William Shakespeare. I played the part of Celia and I signed my lines in BSL."

"How did it go?" asked Perky.

"Well, I won an award for my performance!" said Rose, beaming with joy at the memory.

Perky and Dev gave Rose her own standing ovation with "deaf claps" – and she took a bow.

ANCIENT ACTORS

Mime artists use their bodies and faces to tell a story without using words. Mime began in ancient Greece, when it was used by performers in massive, open-air theatres, where the audience couldn't hear the words spoken on stage.

ROSE'S SUPERSTARS
CLIFF BASTIN

From teenage talent to superstar striker, Cliff Bastin scored goals galore during his record-breaking football career.

SCHOOLBOY DREAM
As a young boy in Exeter, south-west England, Cliff was a talented footballer. In his teens he was spotted by Herbert Chapman, manager of Arsenal FC, one of the most successful clubs in England. Herbert persuaded Cliff to join Arsenal and at the age of just 17, Cliff left his friends and family and moved to London.

RECORD BREAKER
Arsenal fans loved Cliff straight away, nicknaming him "Boy Bastin". Cliff was deaf, so he and his teammates made up secret signs to use during games. At the age of 19, Cliff played his first match for England. He became Arsenal's top scorer and held the record for almost 60 years. This was an amazing achievement, especially since he was unable to play for six years during World War II, when he was at the peak of his powers.

ARSENAL APPEARANCES: 396

ARSENAL GOALS: 178

ENGLAND APPEARANCES: 21

ENGLAND GOALS: 12

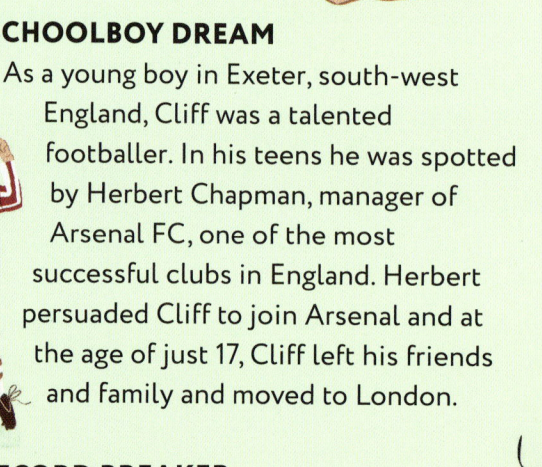

HERO AT HOME

When World War II broke out in 1939, Cliff's deafness meant he couldn't join the army. He became an air raid warden, watching out for enemy aircraft and helping local people during bombing raids. With no professional football during the war, Cliff played in more than 250 "friendly" matches, put on to cheer people up.

THE GUNNERS

Cliff's team, Arsenal, is nicknamed the Gunners because the club was first formed by a group of workers in a military weapons factory.

> *He had a trait few of us are blessed with – an ice-cold temperament.*
>
> TOM WHITTAKER, ARSENAL PHYSIO, 1950

Are you any good at football, Perky?

Oh yes, I was a star WINGER in my youth!

LIVING LEGEND

Cliff's amazing career came to an end at the age of 34 when a leg injury meant he had to stop playing. Football fans in his home town of Exeter never forgot him, naming part of their stadium after him. Arsenal have also honoured Cliff in a series of paintings and photos decorating the outside of their stadium.

STOP 08

DESTINATION: CALLIGRAPHY STUDIO, CHINA

DATE: 206 BCE

TAKE OFF FOR TIME TRAVEL! — PERKY PILOT AIRWAYS

In a flash, Pilot Perky whizzed them back in time. They landed in a courtyard where a man was busy with a paintbrush, unaware he was being watched by time travellers!

"What's happening here?" asked Rose.

"We're in ancient China, at the time of the Han Dynasty," explained Perky. "This was a time when a special form of writing, called calligraphy, really took off."

"Did everybody in China get to learn how to do calligraphy?" asked Rose.

"No, like many kinds of education then, only men were taught the skills," said Perky.

Rose shook her head in disapproval. "Did it take long to learn?" she asked.

"Years! There were over 40,000 symbols and five different writing styles," explained Perky.

Rose watched the man work. In front of him was a sheet of silk. First, he dipped a brush into a pot of ink, then swept the brush over the silk, making a graceful, curved shape. He dipped the brush in the ink again and, with a flick of his wrist, made another mark.

When he finally put his brush down, he had created a row of detailed symbols called characters, each made up of different brush strokes.

"What beautiful writing!" said Rose.

Perky laughed. "Funny you should say that. The word calligraphy comes from the Greek… for beautiful writing!"

"Is this the first-ever writing?" asked Rose.

"Oh no," replied Perky. "People first started writing things down more than 5,000 years ago, far away from here."

"It might not be the oldest writing, but I'm sure it's the prettiest," said Rose. "I'd love to try it. Shall we have a go, Perky?"

"No time for that!" squawked Perky. "Halo may be invisible, but those inky pawprints are not! Team, it's time for take-off…"

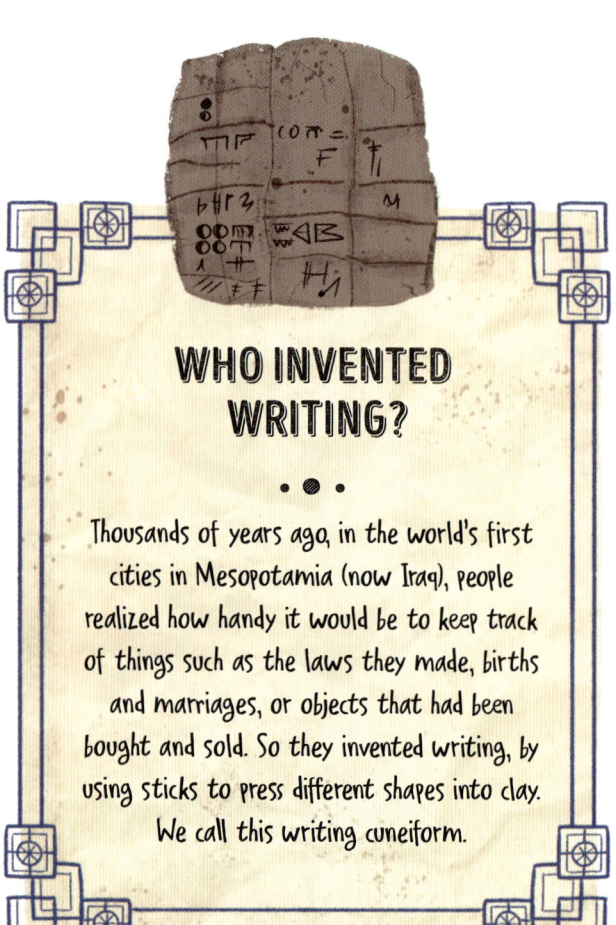

WHO INVENTED WRITING?

Thousands of years ago, in the world's first cities in Mesopotamia (now Iraq), people realized how handy it would be to keep track of things such as the laws they made, births and marriages, or objects that had been bought and sold. So they invented writing, by using sticks to press different shapes into clay. We call this writing cuneiform.

CALLIGRAPHY KIT

In China, the four calligraphy materials – brush, ink, inkstone, and paper – were called the "Four Treasures of the Study".

SCRIPT STYLES

There were many styles of Chinese calligraphy. The two shown here are seal script and cursive script – each picture shows a character that means "dragon". Seal script was mostly used for official documents, while the flowing cursive script was popular with artists.

Seal script

Cursive script

MESSAGING MILESTONES
PRINTING

The invention of printing gave ordinary people access to a world of new information. Instead of copying text by hand, whizzy new machines printed out perfect copies. It became easier and cheaper to get the latest news, enjoy a story, or learn different subjects.

650 CE

BLOCK PRINTING
The oldest form of printing was in ancient China, where text was engraved onto blocks of wood, then pressed onto silk.

1040s

MOVABLE TYPE
Chinese inventor Bi Sheng cut letters into little blocks of clay. These could be reused, so a printer only needed one set of blocks to print any text.

1450

GUTENBERG PRESS
German inventor Johannes Gutenberg's press was a real game-changer! Using metal blocks of type and a special sticky ink, it could print books faster than ever before. The press was a big success, and other printers soon sprung up. By the year 1500, there were 20 million books in circulation!

Have you ever written a book, Perky?

Oh yes! My memoir, "Life as a High Flyer" was a bestseller!

DIGITAL PRINT
Today's presses print digital text created on computers – no more inky blocks to move about. Large presses print thousands of sheets a minute, while small, wireless machines mean people can print easily at home.

COLOUR PRINTING
With this invention, books no longer had to be boring black and white! Presses created hundreds of colours by mixing just four inks: cyan (blue), magenta (deep pink), yellow, and black.

Gutenberg's press could print 250 pages an hour.

Today

1900s

BILLIONS OF BOOKS

The most printed book of all time is the Christian Bible – at least five BILLION copies of it have been printed!

1840s

In cities, children sold the daily newspapers on the street.

INDUSTRIAL PRESSES
The next big leap was printing presses powered first by steam, then electricity. Massive rollers printed on both sides of the paper at once, producing thousands of sheets a day. Daily newspapers meant people could read the news as it happened.

STOP 09
DATE 3300 BCE
DESTINATION VALLEY OF THE KINGS, EGYPT
TAKE OFF FOR TIME TRAVEL! — PERKY PILOT AIRWAYS

Perky was so sure he didn't want to try calligraphy that he rubbed his own wing with his beak! Off they flew again…

They touched down in a land of blazing sun, desert dunes, and huge buildings standing tall against the skyline. Halo looked worried as a passing camel came too close.

"This is ancient Egypt!" said Rose, gazing around in wonder.

"Correct!" said Perky. "Come on, quickly! We're going to visit an underground tomb."

Perky led them to a doorway in a stone building. After going down some steps, they entered a cool, dark room. It took a while for their eyes to adjust to the darkness. Perky handed Rose a torch and she pointed it at a wall. The beam revealed pictures and symbols, covering every inch of the surface.

"Thousands of years before that Chinese calligrapher we saw, the ancient Egyptians invented a way of using pictures to communicate," Perky explained.

"We call this picture language hieroglyphics. Each image represented a word, a sound, or an idea."

Rose shone her torch on Dev as he translated Perky's words. Then she went closer to the wall.

"Look! That lizard looks just like a phone emoji!" said Rose, smiling.

"Exactly. Hieroglyphs are just really, really old emojis! said Perky. "The lizard, called a gecko, meant 'lots of' something – like a big crowd of people."

Back outside, Rose drew her own hieroglyphs in the sand. "Can you guess what this one means?" she asked, pointing to her picture of a pigeon in a waistcoat.

"Handsome?" suggested Perky.

"No, silly! It means 'magic', because you totally are!" explained Rose.

Halo put her paw on the stripey cat picture Rose had drawn and looked up at her.

"And this hieroglyph stands for… 'cute', of course!" said Rose.

SUPER SYMBOLS

There were over 700 Egyptian hieroglyphs, including pictures of people, animals, shapes, and symbols. Each had different meanings depending on how they were used. Hieroglyph messages were read from top to bottom or from right to left.

"Owl" and letter "a"   "Arm" and letter "e"

EMOJIS TODAY

The word "emoji" is a mix of the Japanese words for "picture" and "letter". Created in 1999, emojis were originally designed to save time and space when sending text messages.

STOP **10** DESTINATION
DATE **BAGHDAD, PERSIA (NOW IRAN)**
800 CE
TAKE OFF FOR TIME TRAVEL!   PERKY PILOT AIRWAYS

Leaving Egypt behind, Pilot Perky flew his friends forwards in time by 4,000 years. They landed outside a grand building bathed in warm sunshine.

Perky led the way inside, where the walls were lined with books and lots of people were busy studying.

Perky gave a bow, "Welcome to Persia! This is the House of Wisdom."

Rose gazed at the shelves of books on every wall. "So many books!"

"This was one of the biggest libraries in the world at the time," explained Perky.

"Who are all these people?" Rose asked.

"These are some of the most brilliant thinkers and students in the world!" said Perky. "They came from all over to study here, you know."

"Is this man in charge?" asked Rose, noticing a man in a splendid robe and turban at the front desk. He was busy writing on a scroll, using a feathered quill and a pot of ink.

"Good spot! That's Muhammad Al-Khwarizmi," said Perky. "He's the director – and the world's top mathematician!"

0
ZERO HERO

Zero might seem like "nothing", but it's amazingly useful for doing calculations. It was first thought of in 630 BCE, by Indian maths genius Brahmagupta. He realized that zero was a number in its own right, which you could put with other numbers to make bigger ones. He used a dot for zero; the circle we use today was invented later, by... Al-Khwarizmi!

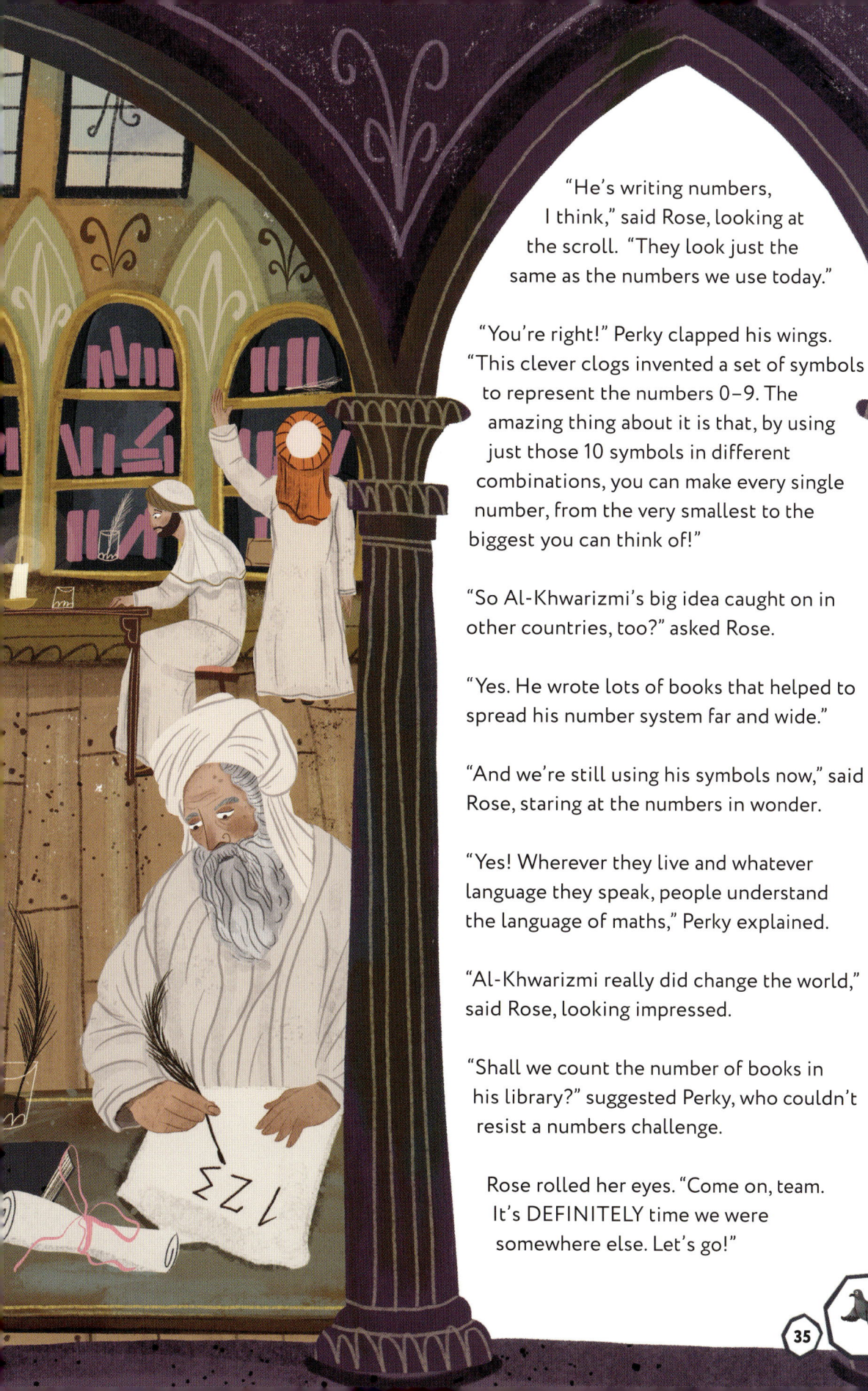

"He's writing numbers, I think," said Rose, looking at the scroll. "They look just the same as the numbers we use today."

"You're right!" Perky clapped his wings. "This clever clogs invented a set of symbols to represent the numbers 0–9. The amazing thing about it is that, by using just those 10 symbols in different combinations, you can make every single number, from the very smallest to the biggest you can think of!"

"So Al-Khwarizmi's big idea caught on in other countries, too?" asked Rose.

"Yes. He wrote lots of books that helped to spread his number system far and wide."

"And we're still using his symbols now," said Rose, staring at the numbers in wonder.

"Yes! Wherever they live and whatever language they speak, people understand the language of maths," Perky explained.

"Al-Khwarizmi really did change the world," said Rose, looking impressed.

"Shall we count the number of books in his library?" suggested Perky, who couldn't resist a numbers challenge.

Rose rolled her eyes. "Come on, team. It's DEFINITELY time we were somewhere else. Let's go!"

ROSE'S SUPERSTARS
THOMAS EDISON

This bright spark was bursting with ideas that led to more than 1,000 inventions during his lifetime.

FULLY FOCUSSED
Born in the USA in 1847, young Thomas loved to do experiments at home. He began to lose his hearing as a child, and later became almost completely deaf. Thomas said that this was an advantage, as he could concentrate on work without distractions.

I'd love to see Menlo Park, Perky!

Let's add it to our next trip!

INVENTION FACTORY
As a young man, Thomas set up a lab in Menlo Park, New Jersey. He and his team developed hundreds of inventions. Thomas seemed to have an endless stream of incredible ideas!

MUSIC MACHINE
Thomas's first invention was the phonograph, a machine that could record sounds and play them back. It was a hit with music fans! Thomas also helped design the first-ever film projector for screening movies.

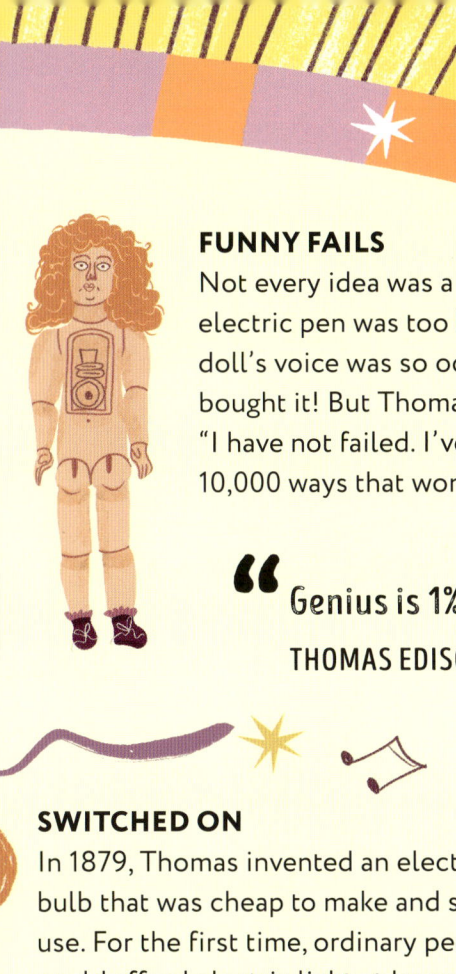

FUNNY FAILS

Not every idea was a winner. His electric pen was too heavy. A talking doll's voice was so odd that nobody bought it! But Thomas kept trying. "I have not failed. I've just found 10,000 ways that won't work," he said.

IDEAS MAN

Thomas became known as The Wizard of Menlo Park because of his seemingly magical ideas.

> " Genius is 1% inspiration and 99% perspiration. "
> THOMAS EDISON

SWITCHED ON

In 1879, Thomas invented an electric light bulb that was cheap to make and safe to use. For the first time, ordinary people could afford electric light at home. He didn't stop there, setting up the USA's first power station. Then he invented wires, fuses, and switches to keep the electricity network operating. What a powerhouse!

LASTING LEGACY

Thomas and his ideas made a huge difference in many areas of science and technology. And, almost 100 years after his life, his words still inspire budding inventors everywhere: "When you have exhausted all possibilities, remember this – you haven't!"

37

STOP 11

DATE 800 CE

DESTINATION ISLE OF IONA, SCOTLAND

TAKE OFF FOR TIME TRAVEL! — PERKY PILOT AIRWAYS

As they landed at the next stop, Pilot Perky had a mid-air collision with a seagull.

"Silly seagulls! Always flying without due care and attention!" Perky squawked.

On this remote island, the wind was howling and waves crashed onto the rocks.

"We're a long way from Persia now," said Rose, pulling Halo close for a cuddle.

"Same date, but a very different place," said Perky. "Welcome to Scotland. Come on!"

Perky led them inside a building on the clifftop, shutting the wooden door firmly before the stroppy seagull could hop in.

"What's going on here?" asked Rose.

Laid open in front of them was the most beautiful book Rose had ever seen. Its pages were full of bright colours, detailed borders, and delicate handwriting. A man, dressed in a brown robe, was working on a tiny illustration of a mouse.

"This is the Book of Kells, a medieval masterpiece!" announced Perky.

They all moved in to get a better look as the man added details to his miniature mouse.

"Who is this man?" Rose asked.

"He's one of the monks who live on this island," Perky replied. "They live together in this monastery. They don't know it yet, but they are making one of the most famous books ever created."

"What is the book about?" asked Rose.

"It's a Bible, with lots of added details and decorations," Perky explained.

Rose watched the man work. Another monk appeared and suggested adding more colour to the border of the page.

"The book is going to be a 680-page blockbuster," said Perky.

"That'll take them ages!" Rose exclaimed.

"Yes, but back when there were no printers, making books by hand was the only way to spread knowledge," Perky said. "Most books weren't as fancy as this one, though."

"It makes me realize how lucky we are today," said Rose. "You can get books on any subject. And they're free, if you go to the library!"

"Times have changed," agreed Perky. "But people are the same. They still love to share information and tell stories."

"Uh-oh! Look who's back!" Rose pointed to the gull glaring at them through the window.

"Ahem. Take-off time!" Perky announced and, in a flash, they were gone.

DECORATIVE DETAILS

Today, the Book of Kells is on display at Trinity College in Dublin, Ireland. The illustrations are so detailed that some can only be seen under a magnifying glass. There are also some little doodles in the margins, showing that the monks sometimes got distracted or bored!

STOP **12**	DESTINATION
DATE	**PARIS, FRANCE**
1829	

TAKE OFF FOR TIME TRAVEL! — PERKY PILOT AIRWAYS

BRAILLE ALPHABET

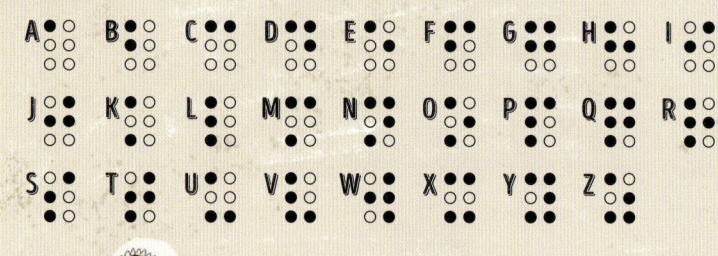

A B C D E F G H I
J K L M N O P Q R
S T U V W X Y Z

At the next stop, they were back in a classroom. But this one was different to the one at the deaf school. There were no laptops, and the children sat at small, wooden desks.

"This book looks like it's not finished," said Rose, peering over a student's shoulder.

"Why do you say that?" asked Perky.

"It's the opposite of the Book of Kells! There's no writing or pictures."

"Actually, there are lots of words on that page," Perky insisted.

"They must be written in invisible ink, then," replied Rose.

Perky shook his head. "Don't look at the page. Instead, put your fingers on the paper and tell me what you feel."

Rose stepped forward and did as Perky asked. As her fingers ran over the paper, she exclaimed, "It's all bumpy!"

"Exactly," answered Perky. "Those bumps you feel are letters, and blind people read them with their fingers. It's called braille."

"That's incredible! Who invented it?"

"This chap here," said Perky, pointing with his wing to the man at the front of the class. "Meet Louis Braille. He became blind as a boy, and taught blind students here."

"So where are we exactly?" Rose looked around her.

"This is the National Institute for Blind Youth in Paris," Perky explained. "The world's first school for blind students."

"So Louis invented braille to help these students read?" asked Rose.

"Yes. Louis published a book about his clever system, and the rest is history. Thanks to him, millions of people can experience the pleasure of reading for themselves!"

Rose clapped her hands with admiration.

"We must take off, my friends! It's a long way to our next stop!" said Perky, flapping his wings and putting on his pilot's cap.

BRAILLE TODAY

Braille has moved with the times and is still super-useful! Refreshable braille display turns text on a screen into readable braille on a special keypad. Screen readers scan text on a web page, then either read it out aloud or print it out in braille. These inventions make it much easier for blind people to use the internet and digital devices.

Raised dots are set out in a different pattern for each letter of the alphabet.

MESSAGING MILESTONES
TELEPHONE

Most of us can't imagine a world without phones, but the first telephone was only invented 150 years ago. Even in the digital age, phones are still the most popular communication tool ever.

1875

FIRST PHONE
When Alexander Graham Bell invented a way to send his voice electronically along a wire to the next room, he made the first ever phone call! A year later, his telephone went on sale and was an overnight success.

1889

PUBLIC PAYPHONE
The world's first public telephone was installed inside a bank in Connecticut, USA. These new payphones were a big help for the many people who couldn't afford to have a phone at home.

Have you got a smartphone, Perky?

No! Technology really gets my feathers in a flap!

ACCESSIBLE SMARTPHONES
Deaf users can make video calls, while those with visual disabilities use voice activation. Users hear descriptions of what is on screen, so they can navigate the internet and use apps.

2020s

2007

IPHONE INVENTION
The Apple iPhone was the first smartphone. As well as making calls, users could access apps, emails, and the internet. When it launched, some people queued for days to buy one. More than six million were sold in its first year.

1970s

MOBILE LAUNCH
The first handheld phone without cables or cords was huge – and much too expensive for most people! It weighed 1 kg (2.5 lb) and took 10 hours to charge. No wonder its nickname was "the Brick"!

1963

TOUCH-TONE PHONES
The first home phones had a circular dial that you had to turn for each digit in the phone number. Then came push-button keypads, which were easier to use, especially for people who were older or who had disabilities.

1964

TELETYPEWRITER
The "TTY" enabled deaf people and those with speech difficulties to make and receive calls. Typed letters were sent through a normal telephone line to another TTY, where they appeared as letters on a screen.

STOP 13

DESTINATION
GREAT PLAINS OF NORTH AMERICA

DATE
1610

TAKE OFF FOR TIME TRAVEL!   PERKY PILOT AIRWAYS

Pilot Perky and the gang left France in a puff of smoke and arrived at the next stop in an even bigger one!

"Where are we now, Perky?" asked Rose, coughing. "It smells like we're in the middle of a bonfire!"

As the smoke cleared, a vast landscape was revealed. They were on top of a grassy mountain. In the distance, across rolling plains and winding rivers, was a mountain range. The sun was just starting to set behind the distant peaks.

"This is the Great Plains!" announced Perky, opening both wings grandly.

"It's breathtaking!" said Rose. "But who started that fire?"

"Look behind you," said Perky.

Nearby were two men sitting around a campfire. Their horses were munching on grass. One man was using a blanket to cover the fire before lifting it up again.

"Oh, I see where all the smoke was coming from now," Rose said. "Is he trying to put the fire out?"

"No! This man is a Plains Indian, and he's sending a message. Some Native American tribes used smoke to communicate over long distances."

"So what's he doing with that blanket?" Rose asked, intrigued.

"He's using it to control the smoke," Perky explained. "Big puffs have a different meaning to small ones. The number of puffs and how fast they come also mean different things."

"That's amazing! But who are they signalling?" Rose asked.

44

"There's no one here, apart from us – and we're invisible!"

"Wait and see…" advised Perky, pointing at the mountains in the distance.

They all gazed in the direction of the setting sun… where suddenly, a series of little smoke puffs appeared.

"Look, there's a reply!" said Perky.

The men nodded and smiled as they watched the puffs rise in the air.

"But how do they know what the smoke means?" asked Rose.

"Each tribe agreed their own secret code for signals so that outsiders wouldn't understand them," explained Perky.

"I'd love to know what they just said to each other," said Rose.

"It was usually things like 'Watch out!', 'Everything is OK', or 'Send help!'" said Perky. "Messages were pretty simple. You can't get too detailed with smoke!"

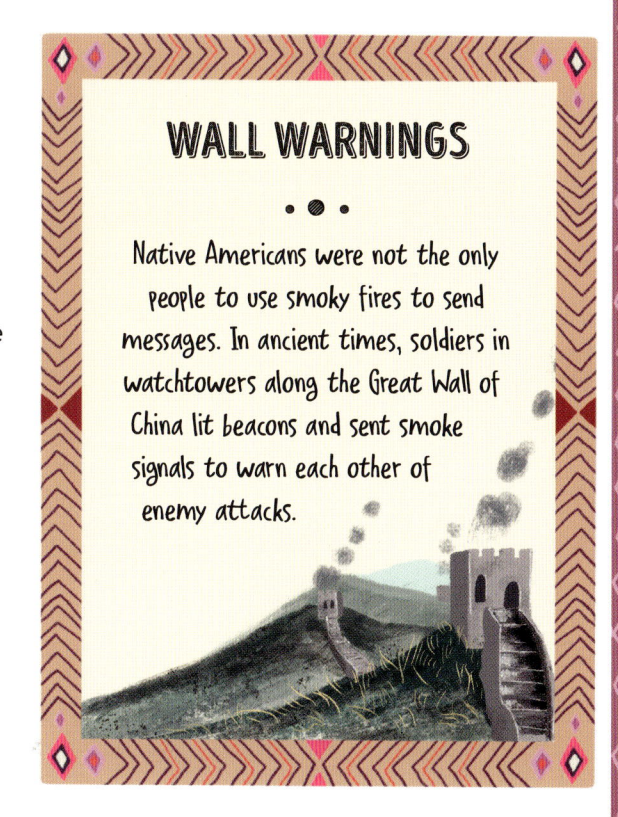

WALL WARNINGS

Native Americans were not the only people to use smoky fires to send messages. In ancient times, soldiers in watchtowers along the Great Wall of China lit beacons and sent smoke signals to warn each other of enemy attacks.

Halo tapped Rose's arm and looked at her with pleading eyes.

"I think Halo wishes the signal meant 'Dinner's ready'", said Rose, laughing.

"Halo always lets us know what she's feeling," said Perky. "Let's visit some more animal communicators!"

STOP **14** DESTINATION
DATE **2024** **MAASAI MARA, KENYA**

TAKE OFF FOR TIME TRAVEL! — PERKY PILOT AIRWAYS

As the team landed back in the here and now with the usual bump, they realised they were in Africa. The sun was beating down on vast savannah grasslands. Suddenly, the ground began to shake. Then there was a terrific trumpeting sound:

"BLAAAAAST!"

The sound came again, but louder this time. The ground shook again, but stronger this time. Halo's whiskers trembled with fear. Something big and noisy was on its way!

"To the jeep!" ordered Perky. They all jumped in just in time as a herd of elephants stampeded out of the bushes and thundered past at high speed.

"Woah!" said Rose. "They're in a hurry!"

"I'd say they're running scared," said Perky.

"How do you know they're not just out for a fun run?" asked Rose.

"Their body language," answered Perky. "They're moving fast and sticking close to each other. Their tails are sticking out straight, which means they're scared and stressed. Their trunks are twisting around as though they're upset. And big, wide eyes are a sign of panic."

As the herd crashed into a clump of bushes, five lionesses suddenly sprinted into view.

Their eyes scanned the savannah as they panted, worn out from the chase.

"A-ha! So that was the problem," Perky waved a wing at the lionesses. "They were chasing down a jumbo-sized dinner!"

At the sight of the big cats, Halo huddled closer to Rose. She didn't want to be their second choice for dinner!

The lionesses gave up and moved off, and Perky started up the jeep. Soon, they were trundling over the grasslands. They spotted zebras lounging in the shade, a leopard dozing high on a branch, and a giraffe chewing leaves off a treetop.

"Slow down, Perky!" Rose pointed to a nearby watering hole. "Look over there! It's the same family of elephants!"

The big beasts were relaxing together, playfully squirting jets of water from their trunks. They were moving slowly and lazily. Their tails swished calmly from side to side and their eyes were half closed. One baby elephant put the end of his trunk in his mouth, as a sign to the other babies that he wanted to play!

Rose marvelled at how the elephants looked so different now. "Bodies speak a language all of their own!" she said.

"I think we should go and check out the body language of another amazing animal," said Perky. "Come on – time to ditch this jeep and get flying again!"

TELLING TAILS

• ○ •

Dogs do body language, too – with their tails! A confident dog holds its tail high, while a scared dog tucks its tail right down between its legs. Happy dogs often wag their tails fast. Wagging to the right is a welcome sign, but wagging to the left can be a warning sign to a rival pooch to keep their distance.

STOP 15
DATE 2024
DESTINATION
INTERNATIONAL AIRPORT, HONG KONG
TAKE OFF FOR TIME TRAVEL!
PERKY PILOT AIRWAYS

The date hadn't changed, but the place certainly had! The vast, empty grasslands had been replaced by the crowds and chaos of an airport arrivals hall.

Travellers scurried to and fro, screens flickered with flight information, and announcements blasted out every few minutes. Cabin crew rushed by, pulling wheelie cases behind them.

Rose's head was spinning! She turned around to watch Perky giving Halo a ride on a luggage trolley.

"I much prefer flying Perky Pilot Airways! It's less hectic than this," said Rose to Dev and Perky.

"This is one of the world's busiest airports," said Perky. "We're here because I wanted to show you some amazing examples of body language at its best."

"Where?" Rose looked around expectantly.

Perky laughed, "Everywhere! You humans have developed lots of clever ways to communicate without saying a word."

Just then, the arrivals gate opened and passengers came flooding through.

"Just look at all the different ways people can say hello," said Perky.

Rose watched people meeting and greeting each other. Some were coming back from holidays or business trips, while others were arriving to visit family or friends.

Perky was right – there was hand-holding, nose rubbing, cheek kissing, and all sorts going on.

"So much love in the room!" said Rose, enjoying all the people-watching.

Perky agreed. "People might be doing things differently, but we still understand what they are feeling and saying."

The reunited groups started to leave the terminal and the crowds thinned out.

"Keep watching," Perky said. "Look at the people still waiting. Their body language gives away so much about their feelings."

Placing hands over the heart is a popular Malaysian greeting.

Shaking hands is a formal greeting in Europe and North America.

48

"OK. What's she thinking?" asked Rose, pointing out a woman nearby.

"She's fed up of waiting. That's why her shoulders are slumped and her head is down," said Perky.

"What about him then?" asked Rose, looking at a young man holding a big bunch of flowers.

"He's feeling nervous," declared Perky. "Look how he's fidgeting with his hair and his tie."

"And Halo?" Rose nodded towards the cat, who was rubbing her tummy with her paw and opening her eyes as wide as saucers. "What's she feeling?"

"Hungry. Definitely hungry!" squawked Perky, as everyone laughed.

BODY TALK

Body gestures can give great clues to feelings. But they can mean different things depending on who is doing them, so don't jump to conclusions!

Folded arms: is he feeling unfriendly?

Twisting hair: she might be nervous.

This person might be deep in thought.

Raised brows: is she listening intently?

Bowing low is a way to say hello in Japan.

Cheek kisses are popular in Europe.

Waving is common all over the world.

Sticking out the tongue is a way to greet someone in Tibet.

Rubbing noses is a Māori hello.

ROSE'S SUPERSTARS
RUTH MONTGOMERY

This inspirational musician and teacher uses art, colour, and sign language to bring music to life and make it accessible for everyone to enjoy.

MAKING MUSIC
It's no wonder Ruth loves music so much! Her dad plays guitar, her mum sings, and her three brothers are pianists. Ruth, who is deaf, started learning piano aged eight. When she was 13, she got a flute for Christmas. Ruth said, "I had a feeling that the flute was going to open up my world." She was right!

INSPIRING OTHERS
In her teaching, Ruth passes on her joyful approach to music. She teaches both deaf and hearing people of all ages, from solo performers to a steel drum band in Barbados! Some of her students have become professional musicians themselves.

FREEDOM AND FUN

For Ruth, music is all about feeling free and having fun. When she was studying at the Royal Welsh College of Music, she loved breaking the traditional rules of music when composing her own works.

TALENTED FAMILY

Ruth often performs concerts with her dad, who is a professional classical guitarist.

STAR PERFORMER

As a solo flute player, Ruth has performed on television and with orchestras worldwide, including the Royal Philharmonic Orchestra. The Royal Schools of Music awarded Ruth two diplomas to honour her outstanding achievements in performance and teaching.

> "Everyone has their own learning challenges. Where there's a will, music will find a way of reaching them."
>
> RUTH MONTGOMERY

MUSICAL MISSION

Through her charity, Audiovisability, Ruth uses visual art, sign language, and music to help deaf people reach their potential – her message is that being deaf is no barrier to making or loving music. As Ruth says, "Music is about so much more than hearing!"

Have you ever tooted a flute, Perky?

Not with this big beak!

```
STOP 16    DESTINATION
DATE       HAWAI'I,
1880       PACIFIC
           OCEAN
🦅 TAKE OFF FOR TIME TRAVEL!   PERKY PILOT AIRWAYS
```

Landing the next stop, the gang felt soft sand beneath their feet (and paws!)

Rose took a good look around. The scene took her breath away! They were on a beautiful stretch of sandy beach, lapped by shimmering, turquoise waters and backed by majestic mountains.

"I think I'm going to like it here, Perky," said Rose, smiling.

"Aloha!" replied Perky, placing a garland of flowers around her neck. "We're on the island of Hawai'i in the year 1880. This lei is the Hawaiian way of saying 'Welcome!'"

Perky popped a lei over Halo's head. She swiped at it with a paw, but gave in when Rose told her how cute she looked.

Some dancers appeared, along with a band of musicians. The dancers wore flowers in their hair and leis around their necks. Although they couldn't see their time-travelling audience, they put on quite a show, swaying in time to the music and moving their arms gracefully.

"Their hands move like ocean waves," Rose commented, watching the dancers in awe.

"Their dance is telling a traditional story," explained Perky.

"Didn't they write down their stories?" wondered Rose.

"Hula developed back when the islanders didn't have writing," said Perky. "So dancing was how they passed on their tales to younger generations."

Everyone joined in with the hula, copying the moves of the performers.

"What do their hand movements mean?" asked Rose, copying the dancers' gestures.

"Different things, like feelings, ideas, or parts of nature," explained Perky. "Hey, you're a natural at this!"

"I wish I could say the same for you!" said Rose, giggling as Perky tripped over his feet.

"You've done a bit of dancing before, haven't you Rose?" said Perky, shaking the sand off his wings.

"Well, I don't like to boast, Perky," replied Rose. "But it's true, I have had my moments on the dance floor."

DANCING QUEEN

• ◦ •

In 2021, Rose was the first ever deaf competitor on the UK TV show *Strictly Come Dancing*. Rose and her dancing partner scored full marks for their tango dance. They also performed one dance in complete silence, to give the audience a taste of Rose's experience as a deaf person. Rose was voted winner of the series and lifted the glitterball trophy!

"In that case, can you teach me hula?"

"I don't think so!" said Rose. "You have lots of talents, but dancing definitely isn't one of them, I'm afraid"

Perky nodded. "You're right. Let's buzz off and find some animals that REALLY know how to throw some shapes…"

STOP 17

DESTINATION HONEY FARM, TÜRKIYE

DATE 2024

TAKE OFF FOR TIME TRAVEL! — PERKY PILOT AIRWAYS

Rose smiled in delight as they landed in a field of bright, sweet-scented flowers.

"What's this?" asked Rose, pointing at what looked like small, wooden houses.

"We're at a honey farm," said Perky. "Those boxes are hives, where honey bees get busy. Let's take a closer look – but we'll have to put our bee suits on first."

Dressed in their protective suits, the team went up to one of the hives. Perky lifted the lid, and they all peered in to see hundreds of bees buzzing busily.

"The bees fly around, collecting nectar from the flowers in the fields," said Perky. "Then they bring it back here to the hive, where they turn it into sweet honey."

Rose held up a honeycomb made of wax, which the bees had made to store their delicious honey.

Perky pointed to one bee, who was waggling from side to side, while moving forwards. Then it circled round and did it all again!

"Is the bee actually dancing?" Rose asked, struggling to believe her eyes.

"Yes, it's doing a waggle dance," said Perky.

"Why? Just for fun?" said Rose.

"No, this bee is delivering a message," Perky explained. "It has found a field of flowers, and is telling the other bees where it is, so they can go there, too."

"It's a complicated dance," said Rose. "Do the moves mean different things?"

"They describe exactly how far to fly and in what direction," replied Perky. "This little bee is like a buzzing, dancing GPS!"

"That's such a cool way to communicate," said Rose. "Look, now it's showing something to the other bees."

"That's a sample of nectar for them to try," said Perky. "They'll find it yummy!"

Rose began to copy the waggle dance, and soon she had the moves down perfectly.

"May I have this dance?" asked Perky, bowing low and bending his wings.

"I don't think so!" said Rose, laughing. "Don't forget I saw your hopeless hula!"

DANCING DIVAS

Bees are not the only animals to strut their stuff. Blue-footed boobies are birds that were born to boogie! The male stomps and waggles his bright blue feet, hoping to catch the eye of passing females.

The angle of the bee's waggle shows which direction to follow.

The length of the dance tells the bees how far away the flowers are.

STOP 18

DESTINATION
LYCEUM, ANCIENT GREECE

DATE
335 BCE

TAKE OFF FOR TIME TRAVEL!   PERKY PILOT AIRWAYS

"**This place looks familiar...**" said Rose, as they crash-landed near a grand building on a gloriously sunny day.

"Yes, we're back in ancient Greece," said Perky. "But we're not here for sport this time. We're going to meet one of the greatest thinkers of all time."

"I thought that was you, Perky!" said Rose.

"Well, apart from me, of course," Perky said. "This is the Lyceum in Athens, the top centre of learning in the ancient world."

In the building's courtyard, a man was standing in front of a group of boys, who were sitting on stone benches. As he spoke, the students listened carefully.

"Meet Aristotle!" Perky declared proudly.

"I don't know how to spell that name," said Dev. "Can you write it out for us?"

Perky spelled out Aristotle's name in the sandy ground, using a twig in his beak.

"Thanks, Perky," said Rose. "I've heard of him. So where are all the girl students?"

"Like most people back then, Aristotle thought girls were not important enough to teach," said Perky.

Rose made a disgusted face. "What a shame I can't tell him what I think of that!"

Perky nodded in agreement and continued, "Aristotle was a real brainbox. He wrote about everything, from poetry to politics. He studied plants and animals, and introduced the new science of zoology…"

"That's very impressive," interrupted Rose. "But why is he a stop on this journey?"

"A-ha! I was getting to that. Aristotle was the first to have the idea that humans have five different senses," explained Perky. "Sight, hearing, smell, touch, and taste."

"Cool!" said Rose.

"He realised that the senses were tools to help us communicate," said Perky. "They act like data collectors, whizzing information to the brain, which makes sense of it all."

"Well, I sense that Aristotle might have been very clever, but he didn't know much about girls," said Rose, frowning.

"True," said Perky. "Let's go and meet some people who invented a super-useful tool to help one of our senses work better."

Rose couldn't wait! She rubbed Perky's wing and … **PUFF!** Perky Pilot Airways was airborne again…

SO MANY SENSES

As well as the five main senses, scientists now know that we have up to 15 more. One of these is the body's ability to sense when it is moving. This is what helps us keep our balance, and is called proprioception (say "pro-pree-oh-sep-shun").

Eyes are the organs of sight.

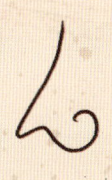

The nose is the organ of smell.

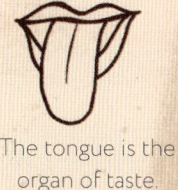

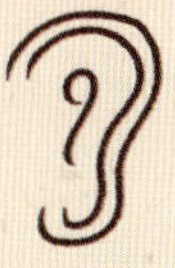

Ears are the organs of hearing.

The tongue is the organ of taste.

The skin is the organ of touch.

STOP **19**

DESTINATION

GLASS WORKSHOP, VENICE

DATE
1284

TAKE OFF FOR TIME TRAVEL!

PERKY PILOT AIRWAYS

"**What a beautiful city!**" said Rose, as she watched little boats gliding along narrow canals, past ornate churches and grand clocktowers.

"Welcome to Venice!" announced Perky, grandly. "City of Bridges, City of Canals, The Floating City – it's got a lot of nicknames!"

"Can we go for a boat ride?" asked Rose.

"No time for that," said Perky. "Follow me…"

They weaved in and out of narrow streets, until Perky stopped outside a building.

"This is the place! Let's go in!" he said.

Inside was a workshop, with delicate glass ornaments on display. In the middle of the room was a fiery furnace, where men were heating glass to make it soft. One man put a blob of molten glass onto the end of a metal tube and blew expertly through it until the blob took on the shape of a vase.

"This is amazing… but what has it got to do with our mission?" asked Rose.

"I'll give you a clue… these craftsmen invented something that would help people to see better," said Perky.

"Glasses?" guessed Rose.

"Exactly. The workshops were used to make ornaments and jewellery, but then someone noticed that looking through curved glass made things look bigger and clearer. So they crafted the first-ever spectacles!"

"Did they look like the glasses we wear now?" asked Rose.

"See for yourself," said Perky, pointing to a pair on a shelf. "Two round pieces of glass were set in wood, or metal, then joined together. People perched them on their noses or held them in front of their eyes."

"Who wore them?" Rose asked, studying the glasses in detail.

"Mostly scholars and monks, who used them for reading and copying text," said Perky. "Later, as more people learned to read and write, and could afford books, glasses became all the rage."

"Now that's what I call a really useful invention," said Rose.

"Absolutely," agreed Perky. "Millions of people would be lost without their glasses – quite literally!"

At this, Halo made Rose laugh by putting on a pair of wooden specs and stumbling into Perky.

"We'd better go," said Rose. "Before Halo knocks into a shelf and breaks all the glass!"

SIGHT SAVERS

Shortsightedness (not being able to see far away) and longsightedness (not being able to see close up) are very common. They are caused by the eyeballs not being perfectly round. The curved lenses in glasses bend the light so it hits the back of the eye in the right place to create a clear picture.

MESSAGING MILESTONES
TELEVISION

Television changed people's lives by bringing the whole world into their homes. Viewers could watch movies, enjoy their favourite shows, or keep up with the news – all without moving from the sofa!

The first television went on sale in 1926.

1926

NO MORE FUZZ
The problem with Logie Baird's TV was fuzzy pictures. Russian-American Vladimir Zworykin used a cathode-ray tube to create an electrical television with much sharper images.

Cathode-ray tube

1934

FIRST TELEVISION
Scottish inventor John Logie Baird created the first moving television images. His mechanical TV was cobbled together from knitting needles, biscuit tins, bicycle lights, and hat boxes!

Zenith Space Commander remote control

1936

TV PLANET
There are 1.7 billion televisions in the world – that's one for every four people!

BIRTH OF THE BBC
The UK's British Broadcasting Corporation (BBC) was the world's first TV company. Three years later, the USA had its first broadcaster, too.

1956

REMOTE CONTROL
Robert Adler's device meant viewers no longer had to stand up to switch channels!

60

VIDEO RECORDING
VHS recorders allowed people to record things to watch later. Before this, a programme was shown at a set time and if you missed it, too bad!

TV SUBTITLES
In the USA, *Sesame Street* became the first children's programme to have CC (closed caption) subtitles, meaning deaf viewers could enjoy the show, too.

1981

1976

DIGITAL TV
Smart digital TVs can connect to the internet and apps. Viewers can watch, stream, or download content to watch on huge, high-definition screens.

Programmes were recorded on magnetic tape.

1969

2020s

WORLD OF COLOUR
Colour TV was common by 1969, and 600 million people around the world watched the US *Apollo 11* astronauts land on the Moon. The *Telstar 1* satellite beamed the live images back to Earth.

Imagine watching the Moon landing live on TV!

I don't want to boast, but I flew up to see it in real life!

61

STOP 20   DESTINATION

DATE **BUCKINGHAM PALACE, ENGLAND**
1902

TAKE OFF FOR TIME TRAVEL!   PERKY PILOT AIRWAYS

WHOOOSH! After fast-forwarding 700 years, the friends stood at the entrance to Buckingham Palace, the lavish home of Britain's kings and queens.

"I'm not really dressed for a place like this, Perky!" said Rose.

"It's fine, no-one can see you, remember?" Perky said. "Let's go inside."

Everyone followed Perky into an enormous room, decorated with elegant pillars and lavish velvet curtains. A very grand-looking lady in a jewelled crown stood on a raised platform in front of a fireplace.

A line of people, dressed in their best clothes, were waiting along one wall, looking nervous and excited.

"What is happening?" asked Rose.

"It's 1902 and this is Queen Alexandra, wife of the new king, Edward VII," Perky explained. "The Queen is honouring that man over there, in recognition of his work."

"Who is he?" asked Rose, looking where Perky was pointing.

"That's Dr Miller Reese Hutchison," explained Perky. "One of his inventions changed the Queen's life!"

"What kind of invention?" asked Rose.

"A hearing aid!" cried Perky. "Queen Alexandra was deaf, and this new device meant she was able to hear some sounds. It was called the Acousticon."

"Wow!" said Rose. "Were there no hearing aids at all before this, then?"

"No, only ear trumpets," Perky replied. "Just basic funnels that collected sounds."

"But why isn't the Queen wearing her hearing aid now?" asked Rose.

"She didn't use it on public occasions," explained Perky.

"That's a shame," said Rose. "I bet deaf people would have loved to know that their queen was part of their world."

The doctor's name was called, and he walked up to stand in front of the Queen. She smiled and spoke a few words before handing him a gleaming, golden medal. The doctor beamed with delight.

When the doctor returned to his place, Rose peered over his shoulder to see the medal. On it were the words, *'Coronation medal presented to Dr Miller Reese Hutchison by Queen Alexandra of Britain'*.

"The Queen was certainly a happy customer!" declared Perky.

"Well done, Dr Hutchison, and thank you from all of us!" said Rose, as she and Dev gave him a deaf clap.

HEARING HELPERS

• • •

The Acousticon was made of three different parts – an earpiece, an amplifier to make sounds louder, and a battery. Although it looks bulky to us today, at the time it was super-cool tech! Today's hearing aids have tiny microphones that digitally process sounds to make them much clearer as well as louder.

ROSE'S SUPERSTARS
HABEN GIRMA

This legal eagle went straight to the top of her class, becoming a tireless campaigner speaking out for disabled people's rights.

NEW CHALLENGES

Haben was born in California, USA. She became deaf and blind as a young girl, and learned sign language and braille at school. She had lots of interests, including kayaking, skiing, and rock climbing. As a teenager, Haben went to Mali in Africa as a volunteer, helping to build new schools.

MAKING A DIFFERENCE

Haben's Mali adventure sparked a lifelong mission to make a difference. At college, she won her campaign for the café to make menus accessible to her and other disabled students. Haben realized she could use the law in the fight for disabled people's rights.

PRESIDENT'S PRIZE

Haben was named a White House Champion of Change by US President Barack Obama.

Haben is completely unflappable, isn't she?

Yes – not a bit like you, Perky!

> You have the power to influence your future [so] keep believing that you have talents to share.
>
> HABEN GIRMA

BRILLIANT STUDENT

At Harvard Law School, with her guide dog Maxine beside her, Haben was a stellar student. She developed her own communications system by linking a computer keyboard to her braille notetaker. Three years later, Haben graduated – she was officially a lawyer!

PUBLIC SPEAKER

Now, Haben travels the world with her current guide dog Mylo, showing organizations how to be more accessible and inclusive. She uses her experience and communication skills to spread a simple message – that inclusion is more than a nice idea, it's essential. If everyone has the chance to fulfil their potential, we all benefit, and the world becomes a better place.

STOP 21
DESTINATION: PUPPY SCHOOL, WALES
DATE: 2024
TAKE OFF FOR TIME TRAVEL!
PERKY PILOT AIRWAYS

The next stop was outside a large building with a sign above the door that said: "**TRAINING CENTRE**".

"This all looks very modern," said Rose.

"We're back in the present," explained Perky. "And you'll love that we are. Wait and see!"

The gang went in and were met by the cutest sight. Everywhere they looked were puppies of all different colours, shapes, and sizes. It was a total fur-fest!

"It's puppy playtime!" said Perky.

Rose and Dev were delighted! Halo, however, looked extremely unimpressed.

"And because it's the here and now, you can play with them," Perky reminded Rose.

Rose got down on her hands and knees to meet the pups. One rolled over and let her tickle his tummy.

"Sorry, am I stopping the pups from working?" Rose asked one of the volunteers.

"Not at all," she replied. "When they are little, pups need as much interaction as possible. The more cuddles, the better!"

"What are they training for exactly?" asked Rose, as Perky flew off to avoid a labrador who had taken a shine to him.

"They'll be hearing dogs for deaf people," she explained. "If they pass the course."

"When does training start?" said Rose.

DOGS WITH JOBS

Dogs help humans out in lots of ways. Guide dogs assist blind people in their day-to-day lives. Search-and-rescue dogs save people from drowning, avalanches, or earthquakes. Other brave dogs go into danger zones to sniff out mines or explosives.

"Official puppy school starts here at eight weeks old, once they are old enough to leave their mums," the volunteer answered.

Rose tapped Dev's shoulder. He was so caught up with puppy playtime that he had forgotten to interpret for Rose!

"What do you teach them?" asked Rose, cuddling a fluffy border collie.

"Pups learn to alert their people to sounds like alarm clocks, doorbells, and fire alarms."

"Clever doggos!" said Rose.

"Cheeky doggos, more like!" yelled Perky as he was chased by a panting poodle.

The volunteer said, "We get the pups used to crowds, noise, and traffic, so they are confident in any situation."

"How do you decide who gets which dog?" asked Rose.

"We match each pup to a person, then we tailor the training to suit the needs of that person," replied the volunteer.

"Time to go, Rose," said Perky, who was being licked by a labradoodle. "Our next stop is going to be even more fun than this!"

Rose looked very excited.
"Let's go, then!" she said.

STOP **22**

DATE **1998**

DESTINATION **JOHANNESBURG, SOUTH AFRICA**

TAKE OFF FOR TIME TRAVEL! — PERKY PILOT AIRWAYS

The gang swooped down over a crowd of people surrounding a stage illuminated by bright lights. A performer in long, flowing robes was singing.

Rose clapped her hands in delight. "That's Stevie Wonder! I can't believe it!"

"You're a big fan, aren't you?" said Perky.

"He's my favourite!" gasped Rose. "A musical genius and a hero. Did you know he became blind as a baby? He's been writing songs and playing instruments his whole life – and I've been listening to him my whole life, too!"

"Have you seen him at a concert before?" asked Perky.

"No, but I do go to lots of other concerts and festivals," explained Rose. "My interpreter signs the lyrics so I can follow the music and enjoy the atmosphere. My friends and I always ask for a sign language interpreter so we get the full experience."

When Stevie began singing his hit song "Happy Birthday", everyone in the crowd sang along with him.

Dev stepped up so he could see Stevie and started to sign the lyrics. Rose looked from Dev to Stevie and back, taking in every word of the song.

"Whose birthday are we celebrating, Perky?" asked Rose.

Perky clapped his wings with excitement. "Look over there!"

A man was walking onstage, wearing a coat and a furry hat in the cool night air. Rose instantly recognized him.

"That's Nelson Mandela!" exclaimed Rose, moving closer to be sure.

"Yes! The President of South Africa is celebrating his 80th birthday along with 20,000 people!"

After he finished the song, Stevie gave Nelson a huge hug.

"They must be great friends," said Rose.

"They have a lot in common," said Perky. "Both of them campaigned for equal rights and peace. And they both love music."

"Look at this crowd!" Rose turned to look at the audience. "Music creates so much joy and brings people together."

"Indeed," nodded Perky. "Music can send all kinds of messages. It can make you feel happy or sad, and every emotion in between."

MORE THAN WORDS

Music doesn't always have words. Many kinds of music around the world are designed to be played on instruments, or by bands and orchestras. Their melodies, rhythms, and harmonies alone are powerful enough to communicate all kinds of feelings and ideas — with no words necessary!

"It's certainly made everyone happy today," said Rose. "Well done, Stevie!"

"He really is a Wonder," said Perky, chuckling at his own joke as everyone else groaned.

STOP 23
DESTINATION: LONDON, ENGLAND
DATE: 1878

TAKE OFF FOR TIME TRAVEL! — PERKY PILOT AIRWAYS

Pilot Perky whizzed them back in time again until they landed outside a shop in a busy London street. A sign said "BASSANO PHOTOGRAPHY STUDIO".

They all entered a large room. An elegant lady in a long dress and a large hat was sitting perfectly still. Behind her was a sheet painted like a garden, so it looked as if she was sitting outdoors. In front of her, a man stood at a wooden box with handles and a thick cloth at one end.

"Why is this stop part of our journey, then?" asked Rose.

"I'm glad you asked that! The invention of photography meant we could record history as it happened," said Perky. "Imagine how wonderful it would be to have photos of those hula dancers, or of Julius Caesar!"

"Totally!" agreed Rose. "Is this the first ever photographic studio, then?"

"One of the first and most popular!" Perky said. "People came from miles around to have Bassano take their photos."

"Even famous people?" Rose wondered.

"Yes, he snapped all the celebrities, including Queen Victoria!"

"Was it expensive?" questioned Rose.

"It was two guineas for 20 photographs," Perky replied. "That was a lot of money, but much cheaper than paying an artist to paint your portrait."

After Bassano had left for the day, Rose spotted a rail of clothes. In no time, Perky was parading with a top hat and cane, while Rose looked a picture in a pretty silk dress. Even Halo was given a lacy cap to wear.

"I'll take a photo," offered Dev, getting behind the camera. With his head under the cloth, he counted down with his fingers.

"3 – 2 – 1…" **CLICK!**

PICTURE PERFECT

Photography provided a view of the world as never before. People could take pictures of their families, share celebrations, view faraway places, and see news events for themselves. Today, about five billion photos are taken around the world, every single day!

71

ROSE'S SUPERSTARS
MILLICENT SIMMONDS

This award-winning American actress is an exciting new star of stage and screen, blazing a trail wherever she goes.

STARTING OUT
Millie Simmonds was born in Utah in 2003. She became deaf as a baby, and learned American Sign Language (ASL). At school she joined a theatre group and gave a star performance as Puck, the mischievous fairy in Shakespeare's play *A Midsummer Night's Dream*.

WORKING WONDERS
Millie's big moment came as a teenager when her drama teacher told her about a film called *Wonderstruck*, based on a story about two young deaf people in the 1920s. When Millie sent a clip of herself to the film's director, he was moved to tears and she landed the job! The movie was a success, and audiences were thrilled by Millie's ability to portray different emotions using sign language.

SET FOR THE STAGE

More success came, including a leading role in the scary movie *A Quiet Place*. It was about a family who had to use sign language in case monsters overheard them. Then in 2023, Millie starred in another spine-tingler – the play *Grey House* on Broadway, New York.

MILLIE'S MASK

During the COVID-19 pandemic, Millie helped to design a see-through face mask that allowed deaf people to stay protected, but still lip-read.

> "There will always be people who won't accept you, but there are others you can find who will!"
>
> MILLICENT SIMMONDS

CAMPAIGNING FOR CHANGE

With her huge social media following, Millie is a role model for young people and the deaf community. She loves taking on new challenges, while also supporting and encouraging more opportunities for deaf people in film and theatre. Let's see what she comes up with next!

Millie was in a Shakespeare play like you, Rose!

Your turn next, Perky! Who will you play?

STOP **24**
DATE **1927**
DESTINATION
CHICAGO, USA

TAKE OFF FOR TIME TRAVEL! — PERKY PILOT AIRWAYS

been printed on the huge presses in the building's basement.

"Let's find out!" said Perky, grabbing one of the newspapers. Rose started to read the front-page story, about a heroic pilot making a record-breaking flight.

"It must have been thrilling to read this story at the time," said Rose.

"Oh, yes! Before everyone had TV, people rushed to buy the latest edition of the paper, hot off the press," explained Perky.

"Where could you buy papers? Did they have newsagents?" asked Rose.

"They were mostly sold on stalls called newsstands, or by street sellers. They stood on street corners, shouting 'Read all about it!'" Perky replied.

"What's going on here?" asked Rose, pointing at the chaotic scene around her.

Perky had flown them forwards by 50 years, and across the Atlantic Ocean, to a newspaper office in the US city of Chicago. Reporters were banging typewriter keys, and telephones rang constantly.

"Looks like it's a very busy day in this newsroom," said Perky.

"Why, what's the story?" asked Rose.

Just then a boy came running in. He was carrying a pile of newspapers that had just

74

"Why is it so hectic in here, though? What's the panic?" asked Rose.

"Well, the paper that got the story out first sold the most copies," replied Perky. "You had to move fast to beat the competition!"

"So you've brought us here to show how important newspapers were before everything went digital?" Rose asked.

"That's right," replied Perky. "Before this time, it was hard to get up-to-date news. Newspapers meant people could read about the latest events, and see photos, too."

"Yes, and from all around the world, not just in their home towns," agreed Rose. She picked up the newspaper again.

24-HOUR NEWS

Digital technology gives us instant access to news. People can follow events as they happen on websites, apps, and social media. Anyone caught up in a news event can be a journalist, too, sharing their photos and videos online with people around the world.

"This pilot was really brave to fly solo over the Atlantic, wasn't he?" said Rose.

"I suppose so, for a human. But we birds do it every day, you know!" squawked Perky.

THE DAILY NEWS — May 21, 1927

PERKY PILOT AIRWAYS TAKE OFF FOR TIME TRAVEL!

FLYING HERO!

American ace aviator flies into the history books

Charles Lindbergh has completed the first ever non-stop solo flight across the Atlantic Ocean.

He took off in his monoplane Spirit of St Louis from New York City and flew 5,600 km (3,500 miles) before landing 33 hours later in Paris, France. This pioneering pilot battled snow, sleet, and fog along the way.

MESSAGING MILESTONES
WRITTEN MESSAGES

We live in a world where we can send and receive messages instantly. But it hasn't always been this easy. For hundreds of years, written communications took hours, days, or even weeks to arrive!

c. 3000 BCE

OLDEST WORDS
The oldest writing we know is from ancient Mesopotamia (modern-day Iraq). Called cuneiform, it consisted of wedge-shaped marks made with a pointed tool, in soft clay tablets.

Queen Atossa of Persia

500 BCE

FIRST LETTER
We don't know exactly when people started writing letters, but the ancient historian Hellanicus claimed that Queen Atossa of Persia invented letter writing. She was powerful and well-educated, so maybe his claim was true!

1635

PIGEON POST
Pigeons had been used since ancient times to deliver mail, but Mongol leader Genghis Khan set up pigeon relay posts so he could send messages all over his huge empire, covering Asia and Europe.

I see pigeons are mentioned here again, Perky!

What can I say? We pigeons are always making history!

PONY EXPRESS
This postal system carried letters all over the west of the USA. The Pony Express was the fastest way to send mail across this vast area of mountains and deserts. Men rode small, speedy horses for up to 24 km (15 miles), before swapping onto a fresh horse and galloping off again!

TONNES OF TEXTS
About 23 billion texts are sent around the world every day.

TEXT MESSAGING
After the invention of email in the 1980s came SMS (texting). This meant people could use their phones to send messages without talking. The first-ever text was "Merry Christmas!"

1992

1860s

2010s

MESSAGING APPS
As well as being a game-changer for deaf people, these apps have made it cheaper and easier to make video calls and send texts, voice messages, photos, or videos anywhere in the world.

1844

Morse telegraph

TELEGRAPH
For centuries, long-distance messages were sent by ship, taking weeks to arrive. The telegraph, developed by Samuel Morse, turned words into electrical signals that could be sent via cables in just a few minutes.

77

STOP **25**

DATE
1950s

DESTINATION
NEW YORK CITY, USA

TAKE OFF FOR TIME TRAVEL!   PERKY PILOT AIRWAYS

A split second after Pilot Perky took off, he landed again.

"That was the quickest flight yet!" said Rose.

"We were already almost in the right place and time," Perky explained. "This is the 1950s, when Times Square, New York, was the centre of the advertising world."

Rose couldn't believe the view. They were standing in a square, surrounded by tall buildings in the heart of New York City. The dark sky was lit up with a dazzling array of neon signs.

Everywhere she looked, lights were flashing on and off. There were billboards promoting cars, clothes, fast food, and the latest films. On the streets, crowds of people were scurrying to and from theatres, cinemas, restaurants, and shops.

"I love it!" said Rose. "When did Times Square first get lit up like this?"

"The first electric sign went up 50 years before this time, in 1904," said Perky.

"So long ago! But these lights look really modern," said Rose, gazing in wonder.

"They don't just look good. They're doing a job," said Perky.

"Businesses can't communicate to every individual customer, so they do it by advertising. In the 20th century, adverts got bigger and bolder… until we got all this!"

"That cola bottle looks like it's fizzing!" said Rose. "Hmmm… it makes me want one."

"Those giant, moving ads were called 'spectaculars'. They were designed to get noticed," said Perky.

"Well, it definitely works!" said Rose, laughing. "Look! A steaming coffee cup!"

Sure enough, real steam was coming out of a huge coffee mug. And across the road, thousands of bubbles were floating from a massive box of soap powder.

"These huge billboards are hard to ignore," Perky said. "You see something big that catches your eye. You think about it. You see it again. You start to want it. Eventually, you buy it. That's advertising – the power of persuasion!"

"Were neon signs expensive?" asked Rose.

"They cost more than ordinary signs," replied Perky. "But for these companies, they were worth every cent. They communicate an unforgettable message!"

"Come on!" said Rose, taking Perky's wing. "We need to make a stop for refreshments. For some reason, I suddenly really feel like a nice cup of coffee!"

BRIGHT LIGHTS

The Times Square billboards used light bulbs that contained a gas called neon. These lights produced super-vivid colours, making them perfect for eye-catching ads. Today, most billboards use LED lights, which are more eco-friendly and cheaper.

ROSE'S SUPERSTARS
BEING HER

Identical twins Hermon and Heroda have double the fun blogging about everything from beauty and fashion to music and travel.

CHILDHOOD CHANGES
Hermon and Heroda Berhane were born in Eritrea, in Africa, and spent the first years of their lives there. When they were seven years old, the girls became deaf. Then, when war broke out in Eritrea, their family made the difficult decision to move to a new country.

NEW BEGINNINGS
The family's new home was London, England. There, the twins learned British Sign Language (BSL) and went to a school for deaf children. They loved being part of a community where they could communicate easily and freely!

SIGN NAMES
Hermon's sign name is "Curly Hair", with a wavy hand gesture. Heroda's sign name is "Long Eyelashes", shown with the scoop of a finger.

FASHION FIRST

After school, the girls studied fashion in the USA and at the London College of Fashion. When they found that the fashion industry and social media platforms did not work well enough for deaf people, the determined duo took action. They launched their own blog, Being Her, with lots of fun-filled content on fashion and travel, as well as a mission to spread their love of sign language.

ROLE MODELS

The twins didn't stop there! Hermon works as an actress, while Heroda is a model. Both are huge stars in their native Eritrea. Wherever they go, they inspire others to follow their dreams and promote their message – based on their own experiences – that being yourself is the best beauty product of all!

> "We never allow being deaf to limit our ambition. Disability doesn't mean inability!"
> **HERMON AND HERODA**

What's your sign name, Rose?

It's "Rose", like the flower, of course!

STOP 26 — **DESTINATION OXFORD, ENGLAND** — **DATE 2016**

TAKE OFF FOR TIME TRAVEL! — PERKY PILOT AIRWAYS

MIAOW!

I'm sorry, I didn't catch that...

EVERYDAY ASSISTANTS

As well as helping people by giving them a voice, speech recognition technology also features in the smart speakers we have at home. They use artificial intelligence (AI) to recognize voices, understand speech, and respond to commands. As well as searching the internet and reminding you to do things, they can connect to other devices to play music, control the heating, or answer the door.

"**I know him!**" exclaimed Rose as they touched down. "It's Stephen Hawking!"

Perky had landed them in a packed hall in the city of Oxford. The famous scientist was giving a lecture on stage.

"Stephen Hawking makes science understandable for everyone," said Perky. "That's why his books are bestsellers."

Dev interpreted the scientist's speech for Rose. During the break she asked Perky, "What actually happened to his voice?"

"An illness affected his muscles so that he couldn't talk or move his body much," explained Perky.

"So how does he speak now?" asked Rose.

"He has a computer-generated voice. Words and phrases come up on his screen and he twitches his cheek to choose the right one. The words are then played out loud via the voice synthesizer."

"How many people use machines like that?" wondered Rose.

"Millions! People can be unable to speak out loud for all kinds of reasons," said Perky. "Technology like this gives them back their voices so they can be heard."

"Do all synthesized voices sound like Professor Hawking's?" said Rose.

"Good question!" said Perky. "They did at first, but things have changed. Now, people can choose to have personalized voices on their text-to-speech devices."

"How does that work?" asked Rose.

"Thousands of people have given samples of their voices to a database called the Human Voicebank," Perky explained. "Then suitable samples are offered to people who need to use a digital voice."

"How do they choose which samples to offer?" asked Rose.

"They take into account things like someone's age and where they live," Perky said. "The person is sent voices to choose from and they pick their favourite!"

"Brilliant!" said Rose. "These digital voices are everywhere now. Dev is always changing his SatNav's voice. You had Bugs Bunny in the car the other day, didn't you?"

Dev grinned and gave Rose the thumbs up as Professor Hawking took to the stage again. When the lecture ended, everyone in the hall applauded the professor.

"We're so lucky that science helped Stephen Hawking to share his incredible ideas and knowledge," said Rose.

"**MIAOW!**" agreed Halo, loudly.

"Oh Halo! We should send a sample of your voice to the Cat Voicebank!" laughed Rose, scooping her up for a hug.

STOP 27 — DESTINATION: SPACE, ORBITING EARTH — DATE: 1962 — TAKE OFF FOR TIME TRAVEL! — PERKY PILOT AIRWAYS

"**For the next leg** of our trip, we'll need a different kind of transport," said Perky. He landed Rose, Dev, and Halo next to a sleek, shiny spacecraft!

"Spacesuits on!" ordered Perky. "Buckle up, team, we're about to blast off!"

BOOM! The spaceship launched and rocketed them into space.

"Come on, we're going for a spacewalk," said Perky, leading Rose out of the spaceship's hatch.

"Is there nowhere you can't take us, Perky?" asked Rose, in amazement.

In the distance she could see Earth, looking like a blue ball suspended in the darkness. All around were countless twinkly stars.

SPACE SOUNDS

• • •

Space is a vacuum, so even if you shouted at the top of your voice, you couldn't be heard. However, built-in microphones on board space probes and rovers are designed to detect sounds on other planets. In 2021, NASA's *Perseverance* rover visited Mars and recorded sounds from the famous red planet, including wind, turbulence, and laser pulses from its own on-board instruments.

Then Rose noticed something strange nearby – a glittery ball!

"What have we here?" she asked.

"This is *Telstar 1*," said Perky, floating gracefully above her. "It's the first ever communications satellite!"

Rose floated closer to the satellite. She could see lots of small solar panels on its surface.

"This is 1962, the year *Telstar 1* launched. It's still in space today, although it isn't actually in use anymore," added Perky.

"Why was it important?" asked Rose.

"Well, it was the start of the Space Age..." said Perky grandly.

"But what did it actually do?" Rose persisted. "It just looks like a disco ball!"

"*Telstar 1* was the first satellite to transmit live television pictures across continents on Earth," Perky replied. "And it also transmitted the first satellite phone call!"

"What a marvel!" said Rose. "It looks too small to do all that! How did it work?"

"TV signals from one place on Earth were sent up here," Perky explained. "Then the satellite bounced them back down to other places, all around the world."

"Are there other satellites like this one?" asked Rose.

"Oh yes," said Perky. "*Telstar 1* was the first, but now there are thousands! Today's satellites are used for things like weather forecasts, scientific research – even the SatNavs you humans use in your cars!"

"This stop has been amazing," said Rose, doing a somersault in her spacesuit.

"Yes, you could say it's been out of this world!" said Perky, chuckling at his joke while everyone else groaned.

85

MESSAGING MILESTONES
DIGITAL WORLD

Today, billions of people can instantly connect digitally, and artificial intelligence (AI) is advancing at an incredible rate. Check out the digital revolution!

MULTIPLAYER GAMES
The world turned into one big gaming community, with thousands of players able to log on to the same, superfast server and challenge each other. Now there are more than 3 billion gamers around the globe.

2005

2005-6

2016

VIDEOS ONLINE
The US website YouTube quickly became the world's most popular video-sharing platform. The first video was a clip of elephants called "Me at the zoo". Today about 3.7 million videos are uploaded every day.

AR AND VR
Augmented reality (AR) games mix real settings with digital content. The *Pokémon Go* game had 50 million downloads in its first week! VR (virtual reality) games use headsets to take players into a digital world.

Do you do social media, Perky?

Yes, I've got my own Coo-Tube channel!

METAVERSE
This technology creates 3-D virtual worlds that people can enter and interact with. The metaverse is a fantastic way for people to train or learn new skills: for example, surgeons can practise new techniques by operating on virtual patients.

2024

2023

SOCIAL MEDIA
In the 20 years since social media first appeared, it has become an essential part of many people's lives. More than 3 billion people are on Facebook, but TikTok is catching up fast, with more than a billion users.

CONNECTED HOMES
New technology allowed devices to "talk" to each other via the internet. Now you can control the heating, switch lights off, or answer the door remotely. You can even keep an eye on your pet and dispense a treat if he's a good boy!

2017

The future

BUDDY BOTS
Robots and AI will play a big part in our future! For example, PARO is an interactive baby seal pet-bot. Studies of hospital patients show that cuddly PARO can help them feel less lonely or stressed.

87

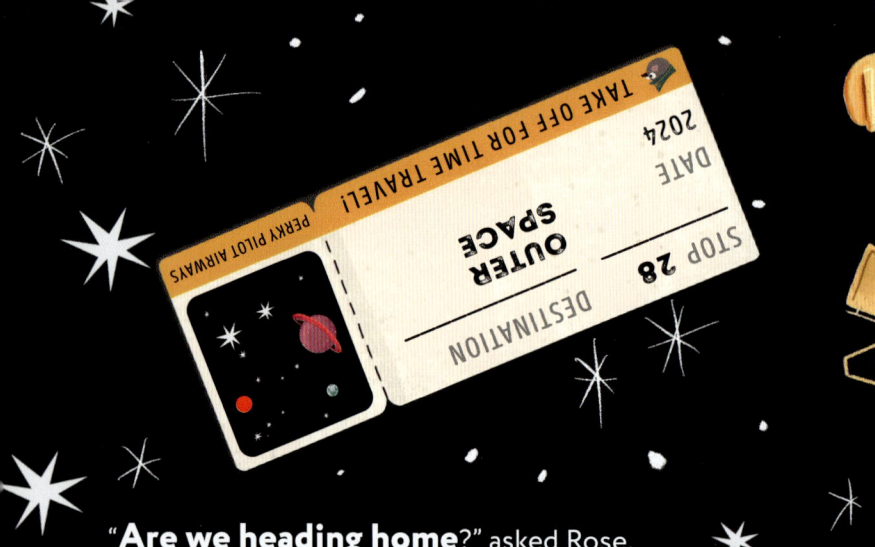

"**Are we heading home**?" asked Rose.

"The opposite," said Perky. "We're headed for deep space. Brace yourselves!"

They whizzed through deepest, darkest space. Stars whooshed by in a flash. Perky was flying faster than ever before. They finally stopped, in front of what looked like a large dinner plate floating in space.

"What is this?" asked Rose, barely catching her breath.

"*Voyager 2*!" said Perky. "This little craft left Earth way back in 1977 and has already been on a grand tour of the giant planets. Look, there they are!"

Rose gasped as Perky pointed out the gas giants Jupiter, Saturn, Uranus, and Neptune in the distance.

"This space probe took amazing photos of the planets, which showed up moons and rings that scientists had never seen in detail before," Perky continued.

"Perky, have we actually left the Solar System?" asked Rose in disbelief.

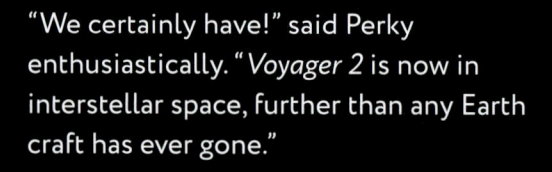

"We certainly have!" said Perky enthusiastically. "*Voyager 2* is now in interstellar space, further than any Earth craft has ever gone."

"What do scientists want *Voyager 2* to find here?" Rose asked, looking around at the endless darkness.

"Life! You don't think we're alone in the universe, do you?" asked Perky. "Probes like *Voyager 2* will hopefully find new life beyond our planet."

"Like little green aliens?" questioned Rose.

"Maybe! We just don't know. The universe is so unimaginably huge that there is potential for all kinds of other worlds to exist somewhere."

SPACE SEARCH

NASA's Exoplanet Watch was set up in 2018 to look for new planets outside our Solar System, called exoplanets. Using telescopes on Earth and in space, they have found more than 5,000 exoplanets but there could be millions more. The more exoplanets we find, the more likely we are to discover life on at least one of them.

FAR OUT!

Voyager 2 has travelled 20 billion km (12 billion miles) from Earth so far – and it's still going!

"Can *Voyager 2* make contact with life forms on other planets?" Rose asked.

"It certainly can," said Perky. "On board is a golden disc packed with information about Earth. There are pictures and sounds from nature, science, and culture. It's designed for other life forms to learn about us!"

"But how will we know if any aliens find *Voyager 2*?" Rose asked.

"The craft is in contact with Earth via radio waves," Perky replied. "So we'll be the first to know if it meets other life forms."

"Oh, I hope it does!" Rose smiled.

"Time to go, people! It's a very, very long way home," Perky announced.

As Pilot Perky steered the craft towards Earth, everyone peered out of the windows – secretly hoping to spot a passing alien spacecraft!

STOP 29
DESTINATION: ROSE'S HOME
DATE: 2024

PERKY PILOT AIRWAYS
TAKE OFF FOR TIME TRAVEL!

The journey home was the bumpiest yet. From the deepest depths of space to Rose's bedroom was a seriously long way!

As they whooshed back in through the open window, everyone landed in a heap.

"Back to Earth with a bump!" said Rose, as Dev helped her to her feet. "And proof that nothing wakes up Rocky and Casper!"

"Journey's end!" said Perky. "I hope you've enjoyed flying with Perky Pilot Airways!"

"Enjoyed it?" Rose said, wrapping her arms around the pigeon. "It's been the trip of a lifetime. I'll never forget it!"

"Where was your favourite place?" Perky asked, hugging his friend back.

Rose looked at the pile of souvenirs they had brought home with them.

"I can't decide!" she said finally. "How can I compare ancient Rome with a Hawaiian beach or outer space? Or training puppies with dancing bees or a Stevie Wonder concert? And everywhere else! It was all totally magical, Perky!"

"And what did you find out?" Perky asked Rose.

Rose thought for a while. "Well, people are amazing," she replied. "We manage to communicate in any situation. In the air, in space, under the ocean… we always find ways to make ourselves understood!"

"Well then, my mission is accomplished," said Perky, fluffing out his wings. "Sometimes you humans get a bit caught up in your digital devices, but really they are just the latest of many clever inventions to help you connect with others."

"What about you, Perky?" asked Rose. "Did you learn anything?"

"It reminded me that communication is at the heart of everything. Whatever moment in time or wherever you are in the world, all that matters is that people can come together to share thoughts, ideas, and feelings," Perky said thoughtfully. "Oh, and I learned puppies are completely crazy!"

"You are a wise old bird, Perky."

"Less of the old, thank you," said Perky. "Now, I must be off! So long, goodbye, farewell, my fine friends!"

Just before Perky took off, he dropped an envelope onto Rose's lap. She watched until her feathered friend had become a distant dot in the sky. Then she opened it up.

Inside was a starry selfie of Rose, Halo, and Perky, taken next to *Voyager 2* in space. And beneath it was a special message that Rose would never forget…

Reach for the stars, Rose! Aim high and dream big. See you aboard Perky Pilot Airways very soon! P x

GLOSSARY

advertising
Making promotional material to appeal to audiences and help sell products.

amplify
To increase the loudness of a sound.

artificial intelligence (AI)
Robotic computer systems designed to be able to learn things, like human beings.

carbon footprint
The amount of greenhouse gases created by a person's daily activities such as buying things, eating food, and using transport. The bigger the carbon footprint, the more harm is caused to the environment.

composer
Someone who writes music for musicians to perform.

coronation
The official ceremony where a king or queen is crowned.

deaf
Describes someone who does not hear as much as hearing people do.

disability
A condition of your mind or body that may make it harder for you to do some things.

eco-friendly
Something that helps the natural environment, instead of harming it.

global positioning system (GPS)
A space satellite that allows people on Earth to locate their position and plan journeys.

Great Wall of China
A 21,000-km (13,000-mile) barrier that was built across northern China in ancient times to keep enemies out.

greenhouse gas
Any of the gases in the atmosphere that trap heat from the Sun. Too much greenhouse gas causes problems for habitats and life on Earth.

guineas
Old English gold coins that are no longer in use today.

Han Dynasty
In ancient times, for about 400 years, the ruling emperors of China all came from the same family, or dynasty, called the Han.

historian
Someone who studies and writes about the past.

inkstone
A stone used to mix ink and water for Chinese calligraphy.

interstellar
A word used to describe the places between stars in space.

journalist
Someone who writes reports for newspapers, radio, TV, or online news sites.

LED
Meaning light-emitting diode, a type of light that lasts longer than traditional bulbs and is more eco-friendly.

Māori
The people who first settled in New Zealand, from their original home in Polynesia.

medieval
A time in history also known as the Middle Ages, which lasted from about 500–1500 CE.

mime
A silent style of performing where only body movements and facial expressions are used to express the emotions of a character.

molten
Something solid that turns to liquid when it is heated.

monastery
A religious building where monks live.

Mongol
A member of one of the nomadic (travelling) tribes that have lived in Central Asia since the 13th century.

monk
A man who devotes his life to his religion, and often lives alone or with other monks.

NASA
Standing for "National Aeronautics and Space Administration", the organization in charge of all the USA's space missions and technology.

Native American
A member of one of the original groups of people who lived in North America, long before people from Europe arrived.

orbit
The route of an object in space around a planet, star, or moon.

Persia
The name previously used for the country now called Iran.

philosopher
Someone who thinks seriously about how the universe works, and why people think and behave as they do.

Queen Victoria
A monarch who reigned in Britain from 1837 until 1901.

Roman Empire
From 31 BCE to 476 CE, the ancient Romans built an empire that stretched across Europe and northern Africa, by invading and conquering other peoples.

satellite
Any object that orbits around a larger one. The moon is a satellite of Earth. Some satellites are devices sent up to orbit Earth and send back information.

savannah
A vast area of open grassland located in a tropical part of the world, which provides a rich habitat for many animals.

scholar
Someone who studies or researches a particular subject in depth.

scuba
Meaning "self-contained underwater breathing apparatus", a device that provides oxygen for divers to breathe while they are underwater.

Shakespeare, William
An English playwright and poet who lived in the 16th and 17th centuries. Shakespeare's plays are still performed all over the world.

smartphone
A mobile phone that also has built-in computer functions, including large storage, internet access, and apps.

software
Programs and operating information that allow computers to carry out tasks.

solar system
A group of planets that orbit a star. Our Solar System has eight planets, including Earth, orbiting the Sun.

Space Age
A time of international space exploration that began in the 1950s and continues today.

vacuum
A space that is entirely empty, without any air.

World War II
A major conflict between many nations around the world, which lasted from 1939 until 1945.

zoology
A branch of biology that studies the variety of life in the animal kingdom.

INDEX

A
accessibility 64–5
Acousticon 62–3
advertising 78–9
airports 48
Al-Khwarizmi, Muhammad 34–5
Alexandra, Queen 62
American Sign Language (ASL) 72
animals 46–7, 54–5, 66–7
apps 75, 77
Aristotle 56–7
Arsenal 26–7
artificial intelligence (AI) 82, 86–7
Atossa, Queen of Persia 76

B
Baghdad (Iran) 34–5
Baird, John Logie 60
Bassano, Alexander 70
Bastin, Cliff 26–7
bees 54–5
Being Her 80–1
Bell, Alexander Graham 42
Berhane, Hermon and Heroda 80–1
Bi Sheng 30
blindness 40–1, 43, 64–5, 67
blue-footed boobies 55
body language 20, 24, 25, 46, 47, 48–9
Book of Kells 38–9
books 30, 31, 39, 40, 41, 59
Brahmagupta 34
braille 40–1, 64, 65
Braille, Louis 41
British Broadcasting Corporation (BBC) 60
British Sign Language (BSL) 6, 16, 20–1, 25, 80
Buckingham Palace (London) 62–3

C
Caesar, Julius 12–13
calligraphy 28–9
Chicago (USA) 74–5
China, ancient 28–9, 30, 45
codes 12–13, 45
colour printing 31
colour TV 61
COVID-19 pandemic 73
cuneiform 28, 76

D
dance 52–3, 54–5
dead languages 15
deaf superstars 18–19, 26–7, 36–7, 50–1, 64–5, 72–3, 80–1
Deaflympics 11
deafness 6, 7, 16, 43, 51, 61, 62–3, 66–7, 73, 81
Deburau, Jean-Gaspard 25
digital devices 8, 22, 41, 75, 86–7, 90
disabled people's rights 64–5

E
Edison, Thomas 36–7
Egypt, ancient 32–3
electric light 37
elephants 46–7
emojis 32, 33
Eritrea 80, 81
exoplanets 89

F
facial expressions 16, 20, 24, 25
fashion 80, 81
films 72–3
fingerspelling 20–1
flowers 54, 55
football 26–7

G
gaming 86
Genghis Khan 76
Girma, Haben 64–5
glasses 58–9
golden disc 89
Great Plains (USA) 44–5
Great Wall of China 45
Greeks, ancient 10–11, 17, 25, 56–7
guide dogs 65, 66–7
Gutenberg, Johannes 30

H
hand gestures or signals 16, 17, 20, 22, 23
Hawaii 52–3
Hawking, Stephen 82–3
hearing 57
hearing aids 62–3
hearing dogs 66–7
hieroglyphs 32
Hong Kong 48–9
House of Wisdom (Baghdad) 34–5
hula dance 53
Human Voicebank 82–3
Hutchinson, Dr Miller Reese 62

I
illustrations 38–9
internet 41, 61, 87
inventors 36–7
Iona, Isle of (Scotland) 38–9
iPhones 43
Italian language 14–15

J, K, L
Johannesburg (South Africa) 68–9
journalism 74–5
kisses 49
languages 14–15
Latin 13, 14–15
lei 52

94

lenses 59
letters 76
lip-reading 18, 73
London (England) 62–3, 70–1
longsightedness 59
Lyceum (Athens) 56–7

M
Maasai Mara (Kenya) 46–7
Mandela, Nelson 68–9
manuscripts, illuminated 38–9
mathematics 34–5
Mesopotamia 28, 76
metaverse 87
microphones 63
mime 24–5
mobile phones 43
monks 16, 38–9, 59
Montgomery, Ruth 50–1
Moon landings 61
Morse, Samuel 77
music 50–1, 68–9

N
National Institute for Blind Youth (Paris) 41
Native Americans 44–5
neon lights 79
New York City (USA) 78–9
newspapers 31, 74–5
number systems 34–5

O
Obama, Barack 64
Olympic Games 10–11
O'Neil, Kitty 18–19
Oxford (England) 82–3

P
Paralympics 11
Paris (France) 24–5, 40–1
PARO robot 87
Persia 34–5, 76

photography 70–1
Pierrot 24–5
pigeon post 76
Pony Express 77
postal system 76–7
presses, printing 30, 31

R
remote controls 60
rights campaigns 64–5, 69, 73
robots 87
Romans, ancient 12–13
Rome (Italy) 14–15

S
Sanskrit 15
satellites 84–5
scuba diving 22–3
search and rescue dogs 67
secret messages 12–13, 45
senses 57
Shakespeare, William 25, 72
shortsightedness 59
sight 57, 58–9
sign language 16–17, 20–1, 23, 50, 64, 72, 73, 81
sign language interpreters 8, 68
sign names 20–1
Simmonds, Millicent 72–3
smart homes 82, 87
smartphones 43
smoke signals 44–5
social media 75, 81, 87
Socrates 17
space 84–5, 88–9
speech 82–3
speech recognition technology 82
speed records 18–19
Strictly Come Dancing 53
subtitles, TV 61
symbols 32

T
tails, dog 47
telegraph 77
telephones 42–3, 85
teletypewriters (TTY) 43
television 60–1, 85
Telstar 1 satellite 85
text messages 33, 77
text-to-speech devices 82
theatre 24–5, 72–3
Times Square (New York City) 78–9
trunks, elephant 46, 47
Türkiye 54–5

U, V
Venice (Italy) 58–9
Victoria, Queen 70
video calls 43
video recordings 61, 86
virtual reality (VR) 86, 87
visual art 50, 51
voice activation 43
voice synthesizers 82
Voyager 2 88–9

W, X, Y, Z
waggle dance 54–5
waving 49
websites 75
welcomes 52–3
Wonder, Stevie 68–9
World War II 26, 27
writing 28–9
zero 34
Zworykin, Vladimir 60

DK | Penguin Random House

Written by Rose Ayling-Ellis
Author Contributor Andrea Mills
Illustrator Lena Addink
Editor Rona Skene
Designer Clare Baggaley
Consultant Camilla Arnold
Editorial Assistant Francesca Harper
Jacket Designers Claire Patane, Holly Price
Jacket Coordinator Elin Woosnam
Senior Production Editor Nikoleta Parasaki
Production Controller Magdalena Bojko
Senior Designer Claire Patane
Art Director Mabel Chan
Publisher Francesca Young

With thanks to Helen Peters for the index and Polly Goodman for proofreading.

First published in Great Britain in 2025 by
Dorling Kindersley Limited
20 Vauxhall Bridge Road,
London SW1V 2SA

The authorised representative in the EEA is
Dorling Kindersley Verlag GmbH. Arnulfstr. 124,
80636 Munich, Germany

Text and layouts copyright © 2025 Dorling Kindersley Limited
Illustrations copyright © 2025 Lena Addink
A Penguin Random House Company
10 9 8 7 6 5 4 3 2 1
001–341746–Mar/2025

All rights reserved.
No part of this publication may be reproduced, stored in or introduced into a retrieval system, or transmitted, in any form, or by any means (electronic, mechanical, photocopying, recording, or otherwise), without the prior written permission of the copyright owner.

A CIP catalogue record for this book
is available from the British Library.
ISBN: 978-0-2416-8167-1

Printed and bound in China

www.dk.com

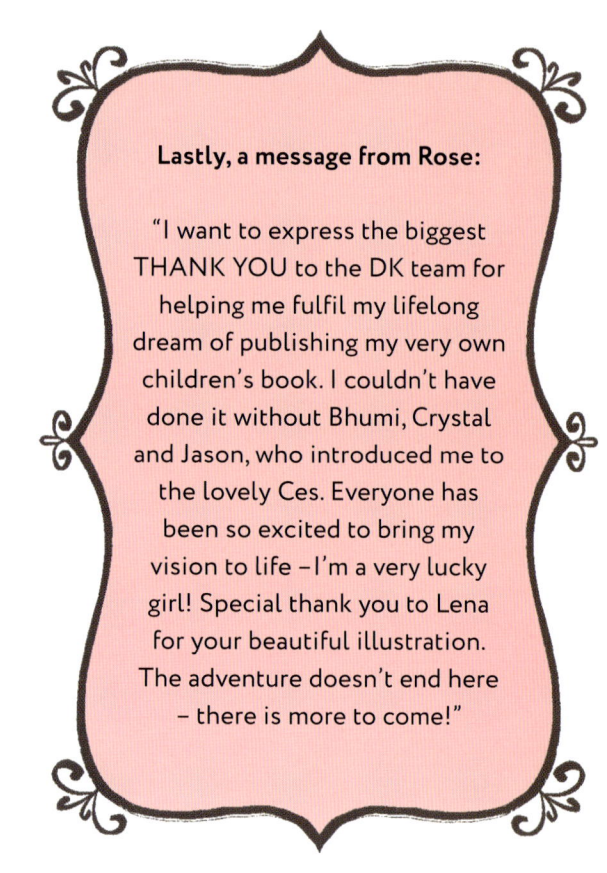

Lastly, a message from Rose:

"I want to express the biggest THANK YOU to the DK team for helping me fulfil my lifelong dream of publishing my very own children's book. I couldn't have done it without Bhumi, Crystal and Jason, who introduced me to the lovely Ces. Everyone has been so excited to bring my vision to life – I'm a very lucky girl! Special thank you to Lena for your beautiful illustration. The adventure doesn't end here – there is more to come!"

On page 14, the languages on the board are: Italian, English, German, Japanese, Polish, French, and Spanish.

How many did you guess?

MIX
Paper | Supporting responsible forestry
FSC™ C018179

This book was made with Forest Stewardship Council™ certified paper – one small step in DK's commitment to a sustainable future. Learn more at www.dk.com/uk/information/sustainability